THE CALIFORNIA DIRECTORY OF
FINE WINERIES

NINTH EDITION

THE CALIFORNIA DIRECTORY OF
FINE WINERIES

CHERYL CRABTREE AND
DANIEL MANGIN, WRITERS

ROBERT HOLMES, PHOTOGRAPHER

TOM SILBERKLEIT, EDITOR AND PUBLISHER

WINE HOUSE PRESS

CONTENTS

INTRODUCTION

Whether you are a visitor or a native seeking the ultimate chalice of nectar from the grape, navigating Northern California's wine country can be intimidating. Hundreds of wineries —from glamorous estates to converted barns, from nationally recognized labels to hidden gems— are found throughout Napa and Sonoma. The challenge is deciding where to go and how to plan a trip. This book will be your indispensable traveling companion.

The fifty-six wineries in this fully updated, ninth edition of *The California Directory of Fine Wineries* are known for producing some of the world's most admired wines. From the moment you walk in the door of these wineries, you will be greeted like a guest and invited to sample at a relaxing, leisurely tempo. Although the quality of the winemaker's art is of paramount importance, the wineries are notable as tourist destinations. Many boast award-winning contemporary architecture, while others are housed in lovingly preserved historical structures. Some have galleries featuring museum-quality artwork by local and international artists or exhibits focusing on the region's past and the history of winemaking. You will also enjoy taking informative behind-the-scenes tours, exploring inspirational gardens, and participating in celebrated culinary programs. Many wineries require reservations for tastings, and with a bit of planning, you can arrange to take part in a barrel sampling, a blending seminar, or a grape stomping.

As you explore this magnificent region, you'll encounter some of California's most appealing scenery and attractions—mountain ranges, rugged coastline, pastures with majestic oak trees, abundant parkland, renowned spas, and historic towns. Use the information in this book to plan your trip, and be sure to stop along the way and take in the sights. You have my promise that traveling to your destination will be as pleasurable as the wine tasted upon your welcome.

—Tom Silberkleit
Editor and Publisher
Wine House Press
Sonoma, California

THE ETIQUETTE OF WINE TASTING

Most of the wineries profiled in this book offer amenities ranging from lush gardens to art exhibitions, but their main attraction is the tasting room. This is where winery employees get a chance to share their products and knowledge with consumers, in hopes of establishing a lifelong relationship. They are there to please.

Yet, for some visitors, the ritual of tasting fine wines can be intimidating. Perhaps it's because swirling wine and using a spit bucket seem to be unnatural acts. But with a few tips, even a first-time taster can enjoy the experience. After all, the point of tasting is to enhance your knowledge by learning the differences among varieties of wines, styles of winemaking, and appellations.

A list of available wines is usually posted, beginning with whites and ending with the heaviest reds or, if available, dessert wines. Look for the tasting notes, which are typically set out on the counter; refer to them as you taste each wine. A number of wineries charge a tasting fee for four or five wines of your choosing or for a "flight"—most often several preselected wines. In any event, the tasting process is the same.

After you are served, hold the stem of the glass with your thumb and as many fingers as you need to maintain control. Lift the glass up to the light and note the color and intensity of the wine. Good wines tend to be bright, with the color fading near the rim. Next, gently swirl the wine in the glass. Observe how much of the wine adheres to the sides of the glass. If lines—called legs—are visible, the wine is viscous, indicating body or weight as well as a high alcohol content. Now, tip the glass to about a 45-degree angle, take a short sniff, and concentrate on the aromas. Swirl the wine again to aerate it, releasing additional aromas. Take another sniff and see if the "bouquet" reminds you of anything—rose petals, citrus fruit, or a freshly ironed pillowcase, for example—that will help you identify the aroma.

Finally, take a sip and swirl the wine around your tongue, letting your taste buds pick up all the flavors. The wine may remind you of honey or cherries or mint—as with the "nosing," try to make as many associations as you can. Then spit the wine into the bucket on the counter. Afterward, notice how long the flavor stays in your mouth; a long finish is the ideal. If you don't want another taste, just pour the wine remaining in your glass into the bucket and move on. Remember, the more you spit or pour out, the more wines you will enjoy sampling.

The next level of tasting involves food-and-wine pairings. In these sessions, appetizers—or perhaps cheeses, nuts, dried fruit, or charcuterie—are paired with a flight presented in the recommended order of tasting. The server will explain what goes with what and how the flavors of the food and the wine complement each other.

If you still feel self-conscious, practice at home. When you are in a real tasting room, you'll be better able to focus on the wine itself. That's the real payoff, because once you learn what you like and why you like it, you'll be able to recognize wines in a similar vein anywhere in the world.

What Is an Appellation?

Winemakers often showcase the source of their fruit by citing an appellation to describe the area where the grapes were grown. An appellation is a specific region that, in the United States, was traditionally determined by political borders such as state and county lines. Since the institution in 1981 of a system of American Viticultural Areas (AVAs), those borders have been based on climate and geography. Preexisting politically defined appellations were grandfathered into the new system of AVAs, administered these days by the U.S. Alcohol and Tobacco Tax and Trade Bureau (TTB). Using the name of either an appellation or an AVA on a label requires that a certain percentage of the wine in the bottle (75 and 85 percent, respectively) be made from grapes grown within the designation.

AVAs, in contrast to appellations, are defined by such natural features as soil types, prevailing winds, rivers, and mountain ranges. Wineries or other interested parties hoping to create an AVA must submit documented research to the TTB proving that the area's specific attributes distinguish it from the surrounding region. The TTB has the authority to approve or deny the petition.

Winemakers know that identifying the origin of their grapes can lend prestige to a wine, particularly if the AVA or appellation has earned a reputation for quality. It also provides information about what's inside the bottle. For instance, informed consumers know that a Chardonnay from the Napa Valley is apt to differ in both aroma and taste from a Sonoma Coast Chardonnay. When a winery uses grapes from an off-site AVA or appellation to make a particular wine, the label indicates the source of the fruit, not the location of the winery.

The following are the appellations in Napa and Sonoma, which themselves are part of the larger North Coast appellation.

NAPA	SONOMA
Atlas Peak	Alexander Valley
Calistoga	Bennett Valley
Chiles Valley	Chalk Hill
Coombsville	Dry Creek Valley
Diamond Mountain District	Fort Ross – Seaview
Howell Mountain	Fountaingrove District
Los Carneros	Green Valley of Russian River Valley
Mt. Veeder	Knights Valley
Napa Valley	Los Carneros
North Coast	Moon Mountain District Sonoma County
Oak Knoll District of Napa Valley	North Coast
Oakville	Northern Sonoma
Rutherford	Petaluma Gap
Spring Mountain District	Pine Mountain – Cloverdale Peak
St. Helena	Rockpile
Stags Leap District	Russian River Valley
Wild Horse Valley	Sonoma Coast
Yountville	Sonoma Mountain
	Sonoma Valley
	West Sonoma Coast (pending)

MODERN STOPPERS:
CORK, PLASTIC, AND SCREWCAPS

It's an ancient question: What is the best way to close a wine bottle? Since the late 1600s, vintners have largely chosen stoppers made from cork tree bark. These time-tested closures usually provide an effective seal, potentially lasting as long as thirty years or more. At the same time, they are elastic and compressible, which allows for easy extraction. Many wine aficionados associate cork stoppers with a hallowed ritual, using corkscrews or other devices to remove the cork and launch the wine appreciation experience.

Corks, however, are not perfect stoppers, the main drawback being cork taint. This results from natural airborne fungi meeting up with unnatural chemical compounds (pollutants from industrial sources, for example, pesticides and wood preservatives). The compounds contaminate the cork bark and produce other chemicals that give the wine a musty odor. Contaminated corks occasionally disintegrate and crumble in the bottle. Some corks fail by allowing too much oxygen to pass through to the wine. Cork advocates claim that improvements in the detection of cork taint have reduced the risk of cork taint below 1 percent. However, any risk at all is unacceptable to some winemakers, who now rely on other types of bottle stoppers.

Screwcaps, once associated with inexpensive, mass-produced wines, have grown increasingly popular in many countries around the world. The caps hold in place a seal liner, designed to allow a microscopic amount of breathability for aging wines over time. And they are easy to remove. More and more wineries are using screwcaps with great success, virtually eliminating the occurrence of damaged wine due to closure problems.

Synthetic (plastic) stoppers also offer a reliable sealing solution. They act in the same manner as corks and are removed from bottles with corkscrews and similar devices. Synthetic corks can provide an excellent seal. However, many are not as flexible as cork, and a highly effective seal can make them difficult to remove from the bottle. Additionally, some lose their elasticity within a few years and are not good candidates for wines meant to age long-term.

Choice of stoppers also involves environmental considerations. The western Mediterranean region contains 6.6 million acres of cork oak tree (*Quercus suber*) forests. Bark from mature trees is harvested in environmentally friendly fashion every nine years, and trees typically live from 150 to 200 years. Cork stoppers are natural, renewable, recyclable, and biodegradable. The forests support wildlife habitats, absorb carbon dioxide from the atmosphere, and sustain local workers. Plastic can be recycled, but it is not made from environmentally friendly material and is not a sustainable product. Screwcaps are recyclable, but the manufacturing process requires much energy usage and releases greenhouses gases into the atmosphere. In recent years, stoppers made with renewable plant-based polymers have shown promise, with one manufacturer claiming a far lower carbon footprint than occurs with screwcaps or cork or plastic stoppers. Many winemakers remain skeptical about the longevity of these products, however.

As the stopper debate continues, some wineries are returning to a simple, environmentally friendly solution used for centuries. They sell whole barrels directly to restaurants and tasting rooms, which offer "barrel wines" on tap to customers—no stoppers, bottles, or packaging at all.

THE MAKING OF WINE

Most vintners agree that wine is made not in the cellar, but in the vineyard, where sun, soil, climate, altitude, and water—collectively known as *terroir*—influence varietal flavor. Growers select vineyard sites for many reasons, including sun or wind exposure and low fertility, because lean soils often produce the most flavorful fruit. Based on the *terroir*, they plant varietals and clones (also called subvarietals) that will grow best, and then wait three years or longer for the vines to mature before ever selling a wine made from their grapes.

Harvest brings intense activity, as truckloads of ripe grapes roll into the winery, ready to be crushed and destemmed. After crush, white grapes are pressed, and their juice sent to barrels or stainless-steel tanks for fermentation, while red grapes are fermented with skins and seeds to provide additional color and flavor. Winemakers introduce commercially grown yeast or sometimes rely on ambient wild yeast to trigger fermentation, a roiling process during which yeast converts grape sugar into alcohol and carbon dioxide. Fermentation stops when the yeast runs out of sugar, which results in a dry wine. Conversely, the winemaker may quickly chill the wine, killing the yeast and leaving behind a little residual sugar for sweetness.

After fermentation, many wines spend from a few months to a year or more in oak barrels where they develop complexity and absorb hints of the toasted interior of the barrel itself. Red wines usually rest in the barrel longer than whites. Most rosés and crisp white wines, such as Riesling, spend little or no time in barrels.

Throughout the process, winemakers taste their young wares, checking for signs of spoilage and imbalance. They analyze samples in a laboratory to determine the chemical makeup of the wine, which helps them to correct potential problems and maintain stability as the wines continue to evolve. Prior to bottling, vintners spend hours tasting wine from tanks and barrels to create optimum combinations for their final blends. Once in the bottle, rosés and light, fruity whites are usually released within a few months. Robust reds remain at the winery for several months to a year or so, which gives them a chance to mature and soften before their release.

To make sparkling wine using the *méthode champenoise*, vintners combine a blended base wine—usually Chardonnay or Pinot Noir fermented without the skins—with sugar and yeast. The mixture goes into heavy glass bottles, where a secondary fermentation takes place, giving the wine its signature bubbles. The wine ages for a year or more, and then dead yeast cells are removed in a process called disgorging. A little wine, called the *dosage* (pronounced doh-sahj), often mixed with sugar syrup to balance out the acidity, is added back to the bottle, and a natural cork is wired in place.

Wine lovers often buy several bottles of a favorite vintage and store them in a cellar or cool closet. That way, they can open a bottle every year or so, and enjoy the subtle flavor shifts as the wine continues to mature over time.

THE ART OF BARREL MAKING

Since ancient times, skilled artisans, called coopers, have made an array of casks for many purposes, including storage and shipping. Dry casks, often crafted of pine and cedar, held tobacco, flour, and other dry goods. A barrel is a cask designed to hold liquids, including wine. Handmade barrels reflect the highest form of the art of cooperage.

Until recent decades, French oak prevailed as the best type of wood for wine storage. During the Napoleonic era, the French planted a number of oak forests to supply the shipbuilding industry. Each forest produced trees with divergent character traits, and barrels made of wood from certain forests had distinct effects on the wine stored within them. In the early years of the U.S. wine industry, American oak seemed to overpower wine flavor. However, research determined that the strong influence came from the way people were preparing the wood and building the barrels. Today many wineries use American oak barrels, which are typically more affordable than their French counterparts. Some wineries also seek out Hungarian oak barrels, which yield distinctive flavors at a lower price point than French and American.

Barrel making begins with experts choosing high-quality wood by looking at tree shapes, growing conditions, and wood grain, as well as the presence of tannins, compounds that influence the flavor of wine. The best wood usually comes from older trees, more than a hundred years of age and at least five feet in diameter. Ideal wood should be straight and have no knots or burrs, and only traces of sap and regular rings. Workers split the logs into staves by hand, to avoid damage to veins in the wood grain, which could cause leakage in barrels. Then they plane the staves and store them outdoors in tiers for about three years to age naturally in wet and dry weather. This allows the wood to mellow out elements that could overpower the wine, such as tannins, scents, and impurities. Winemakers often choose barrels made of tough, porous white oak, which usually matures well in these conditions. When the staves are ready, they are cut and prepared for the cooper.

Barrels take about eight hours to complete. The cooper begins by "raising the barrel"—he takes premium staves and places them in a jig, a metal hoop that holds the staves fast. He pushes three hoops into place and waters the staves, then "toasts" them on a fire to the desired type to suit the wine grape and style: typically light, medium, or heavy. Lightly toasted barrels impart more oak flavor, while heavily toasted barrels give wines a charred or "roasted" aroma and smoky, spicy notes. The heat and moisture make the staves flexible enough for the cooper to take a winch and bend the staves into a barrel shape, tie them with trusses, and place the remaining iron or metal hoops around them. He carves a croze, or groove, in the ends to hold the flat, round barrel ends. Then he seals the ends with a dowel and river reed and finishes the barrel with mallet, plane, and sandpaper.

Barrels are heavy—they weigh up to 140 pounds when empty and much more when filled with wine. But the cylindrical shape allows workers to roll and turn barrels for easy transport. Winemakers use each barrel for about five to seven years. At that point, the porous wood fibers have absorbed as much wine as they can tolerate. They also have little flavor left to convey to the wine stored within. Thereafter, many barrels continue to contribute to winery life as planters, furniture, and wine-themed artistic creations.

NAPA

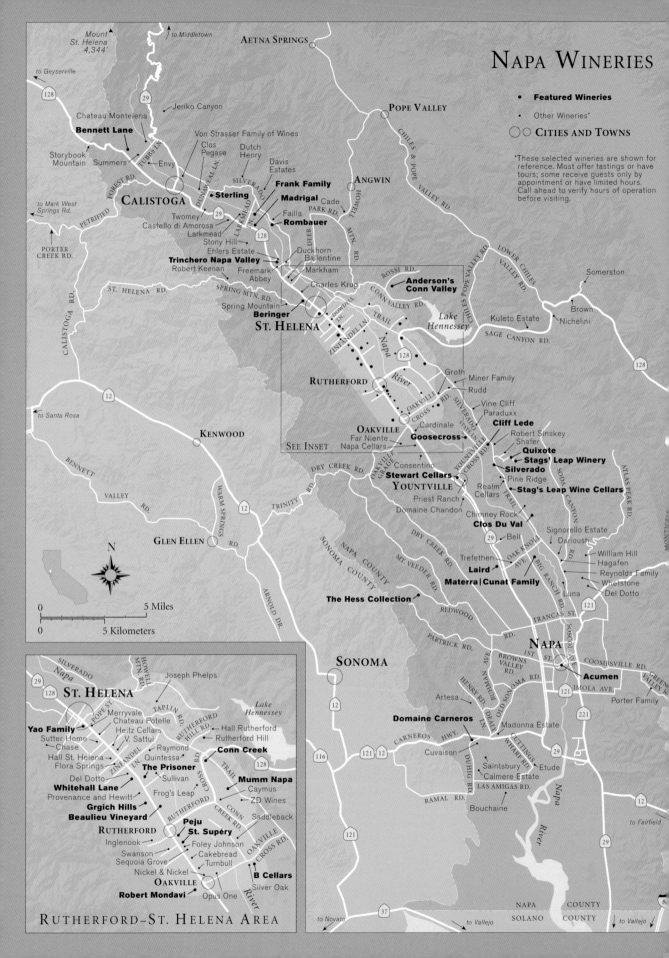

Napa Wineries

• **Featured Wineries**

· Other Wineries*

◯ ◯ **Cities and Towns**

*These selected wineries are shown for reference. Most offer tastings or have tours; some receive guests only by appointment or have limited hours. Call ahead to verify hours of operation before visiting.

Mount St. Helena 4,344'

to Middletown

Aetna Springs

to Geyserville

Chateau Montelena

Jeriko Canyon

Bennett Lane

Pope Valley

Von Strasser Family of Wines

Clos Pegase

Dutch Henry

Davis Estates

Storybook Mountain

Summers

Envy

Angwin

Somerston

Sterling

Frank Family

Cade

Madrigal

to Mark West Springs Rd.

CALISTOGA

Twomey

Castello di Amorosa

Larkmead

Stony Hill

Failla

Rombauer

Brown

Nichelini

Porter Creek Rd.

Ehlers Estate

Trinchero Napa Valley

Robert Keenan

Duckhorn

Ballentine

Markham

Anderson's Conn Valley

Kuleto Estate

Freemark Abbey

Charles Krug

Spring Mountain

Spring Mountain Rd.

Beringer

ST. HELENA

Lake Hennessey

to Santa Rosa

KENWOOD

RUTHERFORD

Napa River

Groth

Miner Family

Rudd

Vine Cliff

Paraduxx

Cliff Lede

Robert Sinskey

Shafer

OAKVILLE

Far Niente

Napa Cellars

Cardinale

Goosecross

Quixote

Stags' Leap Winery

Silverado

SEE INSET

Oakville Grade

Consentino

Stewart Cellars

YOUNTVILLE

Priest Ranch

Domaine Chandon

Pine Ridge

Stag's Leap Wine Cellars

Realm Cellars

Chimney Rock

Clos Du Val

Signorello Estate

Darioush

GLEN ELLEN

Bell

Trefethen

William Hill

Hagafen

Reynolds Family

Whetstone

Del Dotto

Laird

Materra | Cunat Family

Luna

The Hess Collection

SONOMA

N

0 ___ 5 Miles

0 ___ 5 Kilometers

Napa County

Sonoma County

Mt. Veeder Rd.

Dry Creek Rd.

Redwood Rd.

Partrick Rd.

NAPA

Acumen

Imola Ave.

Porter Family

Artesa

Madonna Estate

Domaine Carneros

Cuvaison

Saintsbury

Calmere Estate

Etude

Bouchaine

to Fairfield

to Novato

to Vallejo

NAPA COUNTY

SOLANO COUNTY

to Vallejo

RUTHERFORD–ST. HELENA AREA

Joseph Phelps

Lake Hennessey

St. Helena

Yao Family

Merryvale

Chateau Potelle

Heitz Cellars

V. Sattui

Sutter Home

Chase

Hall St. Helena

Flora Springs

Raymond

Quintessa

Hall Rutherford

Rutherford Hill

Conn Creek

Del Dotto

The Prisoner

Sullivan

Mumm Napa

Whitehall Lane

Caymus

Provenance and Hewitt

Frog's Leap

ZD Wines

Grgich Hills

Saddleback

Beaulieu Vineyard

RUTHERFORD

Peju

St. Supéry

Inglenook

Foley Johnson

Swanson

Cakebread

Sequoia Grove

Turnbull

Nickel & Nickel

B Cellars

Silver Oak

OAKVILLE

Robert Mondavi

Opus One

Napa River

The Napa Valley, jam-packed with hundreds of premium wineries and thousands of acres of coveted vineyards, has earned its position as the country's number one winemaking region. From its southern tip at San Pablo Bay, about an hour's drive from San Francisco, this picture-perfect patchwork of agriculture extends thirty miles north to the dramatic palisades that tower above Calistoga. The narrow, scenic valley is defined on the east by a series of hills known as the Vaca Range and on the west by the rugged peaks of the Mayacamas Mountains, including the steep forested slopes of Mount Veeder. St. Helena, where upscale stores and chic

boutiques line the historic Main Street, is the jewel in the region's crown. At the southern end of the valley, the city of Napa has experienced a boom in recent years, with a plethora of restaurants and attractions such as the vibrant Oxbow Public Market. The mostly two-lane Highway 29 links these and smaller towns that welcome visitors with a variety of spas, restaurants, and bed-and-breakfast inns.

For an unforgettable impression, book a hot-air balloon ride or simply drive up the winding Oakville Grade and pull over at the top for a view worthy of a magazine cover.

ACUMEN

ACUMEN
1315 First St.
Napa, CA 94559
707-492-8336
info@acumenwine.com
acumenwine.com

OWNER: Eric Yuan.

LOCATION: Downtown Napa, 2 1/2 blocks west of Main St.

APPELLATION: Atlas Peak.

HOURS: 10 A.M.–7 P.M. Thursday–Monday. Tuesday and Wednesday by appointment.

TASTINGS: $25 for 3 Mountainside Flight wines; $40 for 3 Peak Flight wines; $75 for Summit Experience of 6 wines with food pairing.

TOURS: None.

THE WINES: Cabernet Sauvignon, Sauvignon Blanc.

SPECIALTIES: Estate, mountain-grown Cabernet Sauvignon, Mountainside Red Wine Bordeaux-style blend.

WINEMAKER: Henrik Poulsen.

ANNUAL PRODUCTION: 5,000 cases.

OF SPECIAL NOTE: Gallery with changing exhibits of contemporary art. Estate vineyards certified organic.

NEARBY ATTRACTIONS: CIA at Copia (cooking demonstrations, food and wine exhibits); Oxbow Public Market (locally produced artisanal products; cheese, beer, wine, and spirits tasting); Skyline Wilderness Park (hiking, biking, disc golf, horseback riding, picnicking).

If the adage is true touting location as the primary driver of real-estate value, Acumen winery scores on two counts. Its estate vineyards, high up the chaparral-laced Atlas Peak appellation, occupy prime terrain for producing Cabernet Sauvignon. Lovers of wines from the "king of grapes" can sample them at a convenient downtown Napa tasting room that doubles as a contemporary-art gallery.

Acumen's founder, Eric Yuan, credits his interest in wine to Bordeaux reds he sipped in Paris during university days. A real-estate entrepreneur from Wuhan, China, Yuan established Acumen with a specific ambition: to

PEAK 2015

create wines steeped in the French tradition yet true to their Napa Valley origins. To that end, in 2012 he acquired thirty-two acres owned by Dr. Jan Krupp, who developed Atlas Peak's most famous vineyard, the nearby Stagecoach. Two years later, Yuan purchased eighty-four acres from Artesa Winery. Acumen reserves a third of its grapes for its Mountainside and Peak portfolios, selling the rest to Beringer and other respected wineries.

The estate's volcanic soils produce grapes with high levels of tannins that Danish-born winemaker Henrik Poulsen, who honed his skills at top wineries in Bordeaux and California, restrains without sacrificing character. Viticulturist Garrett Buckland, who introduced organic farming practices, believes that Atlas Peak's longer ripening times, the result of daytime temperatures at least 10°F cooler than on the Napa Valley floor, allow grapes' flavors to develop more fully.

The collector-worthy Peak Cabernet Sauvignons spend about two years in French oak barrels and an additional year in bottle. These food-friendly wines are intended to age gracefully for a decade or more but are drinkable upon release, a point illustrated during the Summit Experience, for which a local catering company prepares small bites. Summit Experience tastings, which begin with three Mountainside wines—a Sauvignon Blanc, a Cabernet, and a Bordeaux-style red blend—take place in the private, glassed-in Peak Room. Grabbing attention along with the wines is the room's chandelier. Attached to the ceiling by a braided ship's rope, it appears at first glance to be of crystal but is actually test tubes. The fixture is among several offbeat selections by Vincent Xeus, an internationally acclaimed artist who fashioned the swank Acumen space. The Summit Experience and other seated tastings require reservations, but walk-ins are welcome for less formal tastings, as are passersby wanting to check out the art and Xeus's eye-catching design. In 2019 this rising-star winery plans to break ground on a cave and production facility and hopes to invite guests to Atlas Peak within a few years.

ANDERSON'S CONN VALLEY VINEYARDS

ANDERSON'S CONN VALLEY VINEYARDS
680 Rossi Rd.
St. Helena, CA 94574
707-963-8600
800-946-3497
info@connvalleyvineyards.com
andersonconnvalley.com

OWNERS: Anderson family.

LOCATION: 3.3 miles east of Silverado Trail via Howell Mountain Rd. and Conn Valley Rd.

APPELLATION: Napa Valley.

HOURS: 9 A.M.–5 P.M. Monday–Friday; 10 A.M.–3 P.M. Saturday–Sunday.

TASTINGS: By appointment.

TOURS: By appointment.

THE WINES: Cabernet Franc, Cabernet Sauvignon, Chardonnay, Merlot, Pinot Noir, Sauvignon Blanc.

SPECIALTIES: Cabernet Sauvignon, Bordeaux blends.

WINEMAKERS: Todd Anderson, Robert Hunt.

ANNUAL PRODUCTION: 6,500 cases.

OF SPECIAL NOTE: Reserve cave tasting ($65) and private tasting with food pairing hosted by winemaker ($250).

NEARBY ATTRACTIONS: Bothe-Napa State Park (hiking, picnicking, horseback riding, swimming); Robert Louis Stevenson Museum (author memorabilia).

Less than a ten-minute drive from bustling downtown St. Helena, Anderson's Conn Valley Vineyards occupies a niche in a valley within a valley. The location is so remote that most drivers along Conn Valley Road aren't even aware the winery exists. Out here, you could hear a pin drop, except during the busy harvest season that begins in late summer.

Anderson's Conn Valley Vineyards was founded in 1983 by Todd Anderson and his parents, Gus and Phyllis. Gus Anderson spearheaded the lengthy search for vineyard property in Napa Valley. He had the advantage of realizing Napa's tremendous potential before the region became widely known (in the wake of the famous 1976 Paris tasting that put Napa on the world wine map) and before land in wine country became prohibitively expensive.

Joseph Heitz and Joseph Phelps had already established wineries in the neighborhood by the time the Andersons found their dream site, forty acres in the eastern part of the St. Helena American Viticultural Area near the base of Howell Mountain. Unfortunately, the acreage was not for sale; it would take fifteen months of negotiations to secure the property.

Then the real work of establishing a winery operation began, and for the most part, it has all been done by the Andersons. Todd Anderson left his profession as a geophysicist to pound posts, hammer nails, and install twenty-six and a half acres of prime vineyards. That was just the beginning. While the vines matured, the Andersons created a fifteen-acre-foot reservoir and built the winery, the residence, and a modest cave system.

The family did hire professionals with the necessary heavy-duty equipment to expand the caves by 8,000 square feet. Completed in 2001, the 9,000-square-foot caves feature a warren of narrow pathways beneath the hillside. Deep in the caverns, one wall has been pushed out to make way for tables and chairs where visitors can sample the wines. In clement weather, tastings are often held on the far side of the caves, with seating beneath market umbrellas at an inviting arrangement of tables that overlook the reservoir.

The highly educational tastings are conducted by one of the knowledgeable Anderson's Conn staff members and frequently by owner Todd Anderson. A great advantage to touring a family winery is the chance to get to know the people behind the wines and to linger long enough to ask questions that might never get answered during a large group tour at one of Napa's big and better-known wineries located along either Highway 29 or the Silverado Trail.

B Cellars Vineyards and Winery

The lead partners of B Cellars hail from the world of luxury resorts and retail, so it should come as no surprise that guests rave about the winery's polished hospitality and first-class wines and cuisine. B Cellars, which opened in 2003 in Calistoga and in 2014 moved to a twelve-acre former horse ranch in Oakville, achieved quick recognition for winemaker Kirk Venge's fruit-forward blends and single-vineyard Cabernets made with grapes from prestigious Napa Valley sources. To emphasize the wines' food-friendly qualities, all visits revolve around intricate small bites prepared in an open-hearth kitchen in the Hospitality House.

In designing the tasting space winery's architects strove for coated with a faux rust pigment, the bucolic setting. Hospitality clerestory peak ensure an airy feel on sunny afternoons, the sleek and production buildings, the simplicity. Clad in corrugated steel the structures echo and blend into House's large windows and on even the most subdued day; interior positively glows.

The two main tasting options, the Oakville Trek and the Chef's Garden Pairing, take about 90 and 120 minutes respectively, each beginning with a tour of the culinary garden, production facility, and aging caves. Upon returning to Hospitality House, guests are seated and served separately. A recent winter menu paired flatbread, caramelized onions, pear, and goat cheese with five wines, starting with a white blend (Chardonnay, Sauvignon Blanc, and Viognier). Each wine's components accentuated different aspects of the well-chosen ingredients and vice versa. A similarly successful summer coupling involved a critically acclaimed Cabernet Sauvignon and a chocolate espresso–rubbed New York strip steak and accompanying blackberry bordelaise sauce.

Among the most sought-after B Cellars wines are single-vineyard Cabernets from Missouri Hopper, To Kalon, Georges III, Dr. Crane, Las Piedras, and Bourn. Owned by Beckstoffer Vineyards, these six vineyards are among the Napa Valley's most historically significant properties. The prized reserve wines are poured in the private Beckstoffer Heritage room inside the aging caves.

The Beckstoffer and B Cellars relationship is a tribute to the reputation of Venge, whose early wine knowledge comes from his winemaking father, Nils, himself a local legend for his Saddleback Cellars Cabernets. The younger Venge pushes the envelope regarding ripeness and fruitiness, particularly in nontraditional combinations such as B Cellars' Blend 24, comprised of Cabernet, Sangiovese, and Petite Sirah. As with the B Cellars food, Venge strikes just the right balance between opulence and approachability.

B Cellars Vineyards and Winery
703 Oakville Cross Rd.
Oakville, CA 94562
707-709-8787
concierge@bcellars.com
bcellars.com

Owners: Duffy Keys and Jim Borsack.

Location: 14 miles north of Napa, 8 miles south of St. Helena, off the Silverado Trail or Hwy 29.

Appellations: Atlas Peak, Calistoga, Oakville, Rutherford, St. Helena.

Hours: 10 A.M.–5 P.M. daily, by appointment.

Tastings: Oakville Trek, $80 for 5 wines. Chef's Garden Pairing, $185 for 5 wines. Both include food pairings, cave and property tour, and barrel tasting.

Tours: Included with tastings.

The Wines: Cabernet Sauvignon, Chardonnay, Merlot, Petite Sirah, Pinot Noir, Sangiovese, Sauvignon Blanc, Syrah, Zinfandel.

Specialties: Blended wines, single-vineyard Beckstoffer Collection Cabernet Sauvignon.

Winemaker: Kirk Venge.

Annual Production: 10,000 cases.

Of Special Note: First new winery on the Oakville Cross Road in nearly two decades. Lifelike painted bronze figurative sculptures by J. Seward Johnson on grounds.

Nearby Attraction: Napa Valley Museum (winemaking displays, art exhibits).

BEAULIEU VINEYARD

BEAULIEU VINEYARD
1960 St. Helena Hwy.
(Hwy. 29)
Rutherford, CA 94573
707-257-5749
bvwines.com

OWNER: Treasury Wine Estates.

LOCATION: About 3 miles south of St. Helena.

APPELLATION: Rutherford.

HOURS: 10 A.M.–5 P.M. daily.

TASTINGS: Premium, $30 for 4 wines; Cabernet Collector, $50 for 5 wines; Georges de Latour Personalized Legacy Experience, $125 for 5 wines. Reservations required for Collector and Legacy tastings.

TOURS: Georges de Latour Personalized Legacy Experience includes guided walk through original 1885 winery.

THE WINES: Cabernet Sauvignon, Chardonnay, Merlot, Sauvignon Blanc.

SPECIALTIES: Rutherford Cabernet Sauvignon, Georges de Latour Private Reserve Cabernet Sauvignon.

WINEMAKER: Trevor Durling.

ANNUAL PRODUCTION: Unavailable.

OF SPECIAL NOTE: 13 small-lot wines available only in tasting room. Clone (Cabernet Sauvignon) and Reserve Tapestry (Bordeaux blends) available in the Reserve Room.

NEARBY ATTRACTION: Culinary Institute of America at Greystone (cooking demonstrations).

French immigrant and winemaker Georges de Latour and his wife, Fernande, bought their first Rutherford ranch in 1900. "Beau lieu!" Fernande declared when she saw the ranch, deeming it a "beautiful place." Thus, Beaulieu Vineyard, also known simply as BV, was named. Among the first to recognize Rutherford's potential for yielding stellar Cabernet Sauvignon, Georges de Latour was determined to craft wine to rival the French. By 1909 he had expanded his vineyard and established a nursery for cultivating phylloxera-resistant rootstock. For a time, the nursery supplied a half-million grafted vines annually to California vineyards.

In 1938 de Latour hired fabled, Russian-born enologist André Tchelistcheff, who declared the 1936 Private Reserve Cabernet Sauvignon worthy of flagship status. With de Latour's blessing, he introduced a number of practices now considered standard, including controlling heat during fermentation to keep wines cool and protect delicate fruit flavors, and barrel aging in French, rather than American, oak barrels for the addition of more nuanced components. As a result, BV's Private Reserve became Napa Valley's first "Cult Cab" and continues to rank among the region's most widely collected wines.

When guests arrive, hosts offer a complimentary glass of wine in homage to Mrs. de Latour's peerless hospitality. Reservations aren't required for the Premium Tasting of small-lot wines—a Chardonnay and a few reds, Pinot Noir and Cabernet Sauvignon among them. Cabernet Sauvignon is the focus of the Cabernet Collector Tasting in the adjacent Reserve Room, where participants learn about Beaulieu's experiment during the 1980s that tracked various Cabernet Sauvignon clones to determine which produced the best wines. In blind tastings, ones made from strains now known as Clone 4 and Clone 6 consistently scored well. The current Clone 4 and Clone 6 wines, plus an older vintage, are poured, followed by the current Georges de Latour Private Reserve Cabernet Sauvignon.

Guests wanting to investigate Private Reserve more fully can customize a flight of vintages from 1969 on as part of the Georges de Latour Personalized Legacy Experience. The tasting unfolds in a private space within the Reserve Room, whose fieldstone walls mimic those of BV's core winery, built in 1885. In a cozy side room, a glass-topped table displays bottles representing singular moments in the winery's history, including a release of Pure Altar Wine vinified during Prohibition. A brilliant businessman, de Latour prospered despite grape shortages, insect infestations, and Prohibition. More than a century later, Beaulieu Vineyard reigns as a leader in the production of acclaimed Cabernet Sauvignon and is among the longest continually operating wineries in Napa Valley.

BENNETT LANE WINERY

BENNETT LANE WINERY
3340 Hwy. 128
Calistoga, CA 94515
877-629-6272
info@bennettlane.com
bennettlane.com

OWNERS: Randy and
Lisa Lynch.

LOCATION: About 2 miles
north of Calistoga.

APPELLATION: Napa Valley.

HOURS: 10 A.M.–5:30 P.M.
daily, by appointment.

TASTINGS: $20 for 4 wines;
$30 for seated tasting;
$40 for reserve flight.

TOURS: Daily, by
appointment.

THE WINES: Cabernet
Sauvignon, Chardonnay,
Maximus (red blend),
White Maximus
(white blend).

SPECIALTIES: Cabernet
Sauvignon, Maximus.

WINEMAKER: Rob Hunter.

ANNUAL PRODUCTION:
12,000 cases.

OF SPECIAL NOTE: Varietals
Fruit Flavor Custom
Blend Experience, by
appointment ($225 per
person) and including a
tour and tasting of current
releases, allows visitors
to create and bottle their
own wine. Annual events
include Cabernet Release
Weekend (February).
Reserve Chardonnay and
Syrah available only in
tasting room.

NEARBY ATTRACTIONS:
Old Faithful Geyser of
California; Robert Louis
Stevenson State Park
(hiking).

Far from the din and traffic of central Napa Valley, Bennett Lane Winery lures adventuresome Cabernet Sauvignon lovers to the northernmost wedge of the valley, where the Vaca Range meets the Mayacamas Mountains. This sequestered setting just north of the town of Calistoga features dramatic views of Mount St. Helena and the palisades, which provide an ideal backdrop for Bennett Lane's handcrafted, small-lot wines. Bennett Lane's signature wine is named Maximus, after the second-century Roman emperor Magnus Maximus, a noted vinophile of his day. The exact percentages of varietals that go into the Maximus wines vary somewhat from vintage to vintage. The Maximus Red Feasting Wine is a unique blend, made primarily from

Cabernet Sauvignon, with or so Merlot, as well as a sometimes, Petit Verdot. At the name of the game, and about this elusive art are program whereby they taste varietals to create their own the addition of 20 percent small amount of Syrah and, Bennett Lane, blending is tasters eager to learn more invited to take part in a special and combine a selection of Maximus blend.

Visitors to the Mediterranean-style tasting room, painted a rich terra-cotta and topped by a clay-tile roof, arrive via a long blacktop driveway that bisects the winery's Cabernet Sauvignon vines. The structure's exterior evokes a small villa, but inside the feel is more upscale-casual living room, with the Brazilian granite tasting bar straight ahead vying for visual attention with a nearby seating area decorated with sleek leather furniture. Cork wallpaper lines a wall punctuated by a large wooden door that opens into the production facility, one of the stops on a tour that begins in what the hosts affectionately call "the petting vineyard," a demonstration vineyard of Chardonnay and six red varietals.

Owners Randy and Lisa Lynch were relative newcomers to the world of wine in 2003, when they purchased what had once been a custom crush facility. Originally, they had been looking for a second home with vineyard land, and soon after purchasing a residence in Calistoga, they bought the Bennett Lane property. The Lynches were encouraged by critical praise for their wines, whose fruit now comes from highly acclaimed sources in Napa Valley. These vineyards are dotted throughout the valley, from Yountville in the south to Randy Lynch's vineyard in Calistoga in the north. Lynch's goal is to create wines that are both approachable and complex, what he calls "the best of both worlds, meaning you can drink them today, but they are structured enough to cellar for several years."

BERINGER VINEYARDS

BERINGER VINEYARDS
2000 Main St.
St. Helena, CA 94574
707-257-5771
beringer.com

OWNER: Treasury
Wine Estates.

LOCATION: On Hwy. 29
about .5 mile north of
St. Helena.

APPELLATION: Napa Valley.

HOURS: 10 A.M.–5:30 P.M.
daily.

TASTINGS AND TOURS:
Various options are
available. Check
beringer.com for
information and
reservations.

THE WINES: Cabernet
Sauvignon, Chardonnay,
Merlot, red blends.

SPECIALTIES: Private Reserve
Cabernet Sauvignon,
single-vineyard Cabernet
Sauvignon, Private Reserve
Chardonnay.

WINEMAKER:
Mark Beringer.

ANNUAL PRODUCTION:
Unavailable.

OF SPECIAL NOTE: Tours
include visit to barrel
storage caves hand-
chiseled in late 1800s.

NEARBY ATTRACTIONS:
Bothe-Napa State Park
(hiking, picnicking,
horseback riding,
swimming); Robert
Louis Stevenson Museum
(author memorabilia).

With its 1883 Rhine House and hand-carved aging tunnels, Beringer Vineyards is steeped in history like few other California wineries. Established in 1876, at the dawn of California wine, it is the only winery from that founding era that has never missed a vintage. Today, Beringer is widely recognized for combining established traditions with modern elegance.

It was German know-how and the vision that the Napa Valley could produce wines as fine as those from Europe that set the Beringer brothers on the path to glory. Jacob and Frederick Beringer emigrated from Mainz, Germany, to the United States in the 1860s. Jacob, having worked in cellars in Germany, was intrigued when he heard that the California climate was

ideal for growing the varietal grapes that flourished in Europe's winemaking regions. Leaving Frederick in New York, he traveled west in 1870 to discover that Napa Valley's rocky, well-drained soils were similar to those in his native Rhine Valley. Five years later, he bought land with Frederick and began excavating the hillsides to create tunnels for aging his wines. During the building of the caves and winery, Jacob lived in an 1848 farmhouse that today is known as the Hudson House. The meticulously restored and expanded structure now serves as Beringer Vineyards' Culinary Arts Center.

The star attraction on the lavishly landscaped grounds is unquestionably the seventeen-room Rhine House, which Frederick modeled after his ancestral home in Germany. The redwood, brick, and stucco mansion is painted in the original Tudor color scheme of earth tones, and slate covers the gabled roof and exterior. The interior of the Rhine House is graced with extraordinary gems of craftsmanship, such as Belgian art nouveau–style stained-glass windows.

Beringer Vineyards was the first winery in Napa Valley to give public tours and continues the tradition with two signature tours, each covering the winery and its fascinating history. An introductory tour takes visitors to the cellars and hand-dug aging tunnels in the Old Stone Winery, where they enjoy wine tasting. A longer, more in-depth tour, the Taste of Beringer, includes a brief tour of the property and demonstration vineyard, followed by a seated tasting in the historic Rhine House. Guests explore the art of wine-and-food pairing by sampling a flight of reserve wines served with seasonal treats prepared by the winery's culinary team.

CLIFF LEDE VINEYARDS

With pieces in his collection by Jim Dine, Tony Scherman, Sophie Ryder, and other sculptors, painters, and photographers, vintner Cliff Lede qualifies as a patron of the arts. Following his early 2000s purchase of a Yountville winery and two Stags Leap District vineyards, the Canadian construction magnate proved that his knack for fostering creativity extends well beyond the art he acquires.

To design the tasting room and production facilities, Lede (pronounced "lady") commissioned acclaimed architect Howard Backen. Out in the field, he hired David Abreu, a viticultural virtuoso renowned for his meticulous farming and proprietary Cabernet Sauvignon clones from Screaming Eagle and other all-star Napa Valley vineyards. The results: a stylish tasting room, a state-of-the-art winery that blends gracefully into the tree-studded hills behind it, and flourishing vineyards.

Bordeaux-style red wines, the winery's focus, include Cabernet Sauvignons from the estate vineyards, the 20-acre hillside Poetry and 40-acre Twin Peaks on the valley floor. Three top wines — Poetry Cabernet, a Songbook blend from two Abreu vineyards in northern Napa Valley, and a Cabernet from the celebrated Beckstoffer To Kalon Vineyard in Oakville — routinely garner high marks from major critics. Together these wines receive billing as the Platinum Playlist.

Collectors and lovers of classic rock—Lede's abiding passion—gravitate to the Backstage Tasting Lounge, a splashy gallery with ultra-contemporary sofas, Philippe Starck chairs, and rock art and memorabilia. Among the highlights of Backstage tastings is the Rock Block Cabernet, assembled from its vintage's most noteworthy vineyard blocks, which Lede named for his favorite songs. In the 2016 Soul Fire blend, grapes from Heart Full of Soul (Yardbirds, 1968) and Light My Fire (Doors, 1967) predominated. Backstage tastings are highlighted by a selection of Platinum Playlist wines.

Walk-ins are welcome to sip in the main tasting room. A better bet, especially on busy summer weekends, is to reserve a seat on the veranda outside the tasting room or in the FEL Pinot Garden, where the Chardonnays and Pinot Noirs of sister winery FEL Wines, based in Anderson Valley, are the featured pours. A lavish garden and sculptures like Jim Dine's *Twin 6' Hearts* (by far the top background for social media posts), set against a backdrop of stunning vineyards, lend the exterior spaces the feel of a sophisticated Napa landscape. With classic rock in constant rotation indoors and out, the mood throughout the winery remains consistently upbeat, the inspired setting, wines, and hospitality all confirmation of its founder's spirit of creativity.

2014
CLIFF LEDE
NAPA VALLEY
CABERNET SAUVIGNON
STAGS LEAP DISTRICT

CLIFF LEDE VINEYARDS
1473 Yountville Cross Rd.
Yountville, CA 94599
707-944-8642
info@ledefamilywines.com
cliffledevineyards.com

OWNER: Cliff Lede.

LOCATION: 2 miles northeast of downtown Yountville.

APPELLATIONS: Calistoga, Diamond Mountain, Howell Mountain, Napa Valley, Oakville, Stags Leap District.

HOURS: 10 A.M.–4 P.M. daily.

TASTINGS: $35 for 5 wines at the tasting bar, $50 for 5 wines on the veranda, $75 for 5 wines in the Backstage Tasting Lounge (by appointment). Customized tastings at winery and other private spaces, including culinary pairings, available by reservation.

TOURS: Winery and vineyard tours available as part of customized tastings.

THE WINES: Cabernet Sauvignon, Sauvignon Blanc.

SPECIALTIES: Single-vineyard Cabernet Sauvignon. Bordeaux-style red wines.

WINEMAKER: Christopher Tynan.

ANNUAL PRODUCTION: Unavailable.

OF SPECIAL NOTE: Winery and five-room Poetry Inn, overlooking Poetry Vineyard, designed by noted architect Howard Backen. Rotating rock music–related art exhibits in Backstage Tasting Lounge (with Backstage tasting). Many wines available only in tasting room.

NEARBY ATTRACTION: Napa Valley Museum (winemaking displays, art exhibits).

CLOS DU VAL

CLOS DU VAL
5330 Silverado Trail
Napa, CA 94558
707-261-5212
hospitality@closduval.com
closduval.com

OWNERS: Goelet family.

LOCATION: 7 miles north of downtown Napa; 3.5 miles south of Yountville Cross Rd.

APPELLATIONS: Los Carneros, Stags Leap District, Yountville.

HOURS: 10 A.M.–5 P.M. daily. Reservations recommended.

TASTINGS: $35 for 4 or 5 wines; $65 for reserve tasting of 4 or 5 wines.

TOURS: None.

THE WINES: Cabernet Franc, Cabernet Sauvignon, Chardonnay, Merlot, Petit Verdot, Pinot Noir, Sauvignon Blanc.

SPECIALTIES: Stags Leap District Cabernet Sauvignon: Hirondelle Estate Vineyard; Estate SVS (Special Vineyard Selection); and Three Graces (Cabernet-based Bordeaux-style red blend from Hirondelle Estate Vineyard).

WINEMAKER: Ted Henry.

ANNUAL PRODUCTION: 40,000 cases.

OF SPECIAL NOTE: Most wines available only in tasting room. Spring Vineyard Supper Event (family style, farm to table). Basket lunches available (reserve ahead). Participant in 1976 Judgment of Paris tastings.

NEARBY ATTRACTIONS: CIA at Copia (cooking demonstrations, food and wine exhibits); Napa Valley Museum (winemaking displays, art exhibits).

A new hospitality center styled by an acclaimed local designer and a back-to-the-future focus on three long-held estate vineyards have reinvigorated Clos Du Val, among the oldest wineries of the Napa Valley's post-mid-1960s "modern era." Established in 1972 by the Goelet family, which still owns the winery, Clos Du Val made a splash with its debut Cabernet, one of six California wines competing against four French ones in the legendary 1976 Judgment of Paris. The blind tasting, in which the California wines fared well, elevated the Napa Valley's stature as a wine-producing region.

Clos Du Val's French-born founding winemaker, Bernard Portet, first came to the Napa Valley as part of a worldwide quest on behalf of the Goelets for the ideal spot to grow first-class Bordeaux grapes. After reviewing sites from Europe to South Africa to Chile, he chose a 150-acre tract in what's now the southern Napa Valley's Stags Leap District appellation. The Hirondelle Estate Vineyard, as the original property is called these days, takes its name from the French word for "swallow," in honor of the birds that return to Clos Du Val each spring.

Over the years, wine production at Clos Du Val grew ever larger, but in 2014 the Goelets, seeking to reposition the brand, brought in a new CEO, Steve Tamburelli. An industry veteran who'd served a decade as general manager of the Napa Valley's much-admired Chappellet Winery, Tamburelli sold the family on the idea of drastically cutting back production and concentrating on fruit grown in the vineyards Portet had so wisely selected. Most of the wines, now made by Ted Henry, come from grapes grown at Hirondelle, as well as estate vineyards in nearby Yountville.

As part of Clos Du Val's evolution, Tamburelli hired architect Michael Guthrie of San Francisco, known for his au courant restaurant, winery, and residential designs, to fashion Hirondelle House, the new hospitality center. Guthrie nestled the space up against the existing ivy-covered production facility but applied distinctly twenty-first-century touches, most notably floor-to-ceiling retractable glass doors that open up to a patio with an eighty-foot-long water feature and, beyond it, Cabernet Sauvignon vines. St. Helena–based Erin Martin took a similar approach with the interiors, incorporating staves from massive oak tanks formerly in the cellar into her otherwise haute-contemporary scheme. The result is a light-filled space that at once reflects the past but resolutely embraces the future.

CONN CREEK NAPA VALLEY

CONN CREEK NAPA VALLEY
8711 Silverado Trail
St. Helena, CA 94574
707-963-9100
800-793-7960
info@conncreek.com
conncreek.com

OWNER: Ste. Michelle Wine
Estates.

LOCATION: Silverado Trail at
Conn Creek Rd.

APPELLATION: Rutherford.

HOURS: 10:30 A.M.–
4:30 P.M. daily.

TASTINGS: $25 for 4 wines;
$45 for Anthology Salon
reserve tasting of 4 wines.

TOURS: None.

THE WINES: Cabernet
Sauvignon, Chardonnay,
Malbec, Merlot, Sauvignon
Blanc.

SPECIALTIES: AVA-specific
Cabernet Sauvignons from
around the Napa Valley.

WINEMAKER: Elizabeth
DeLouise-Gant.

ANNUAL PRODUCTION:
Unavailable.

OF SPECIAL NOTE: Garden
tastings Friday and
weekends; live music on
Sundays. Barrel Blending
Experience offered daily.
AVA Series Cabernet Sau-
vignons and several other
wines available only in
tasting room.

NEARBY ATTRACTIONS:
Culinary Institute of
America at Greystone
(cooking demonstrations);
Bothe-Napa State Park
(hiking, picnicking,
horseback riding, swim-
ming); Robert Louis
Stevenson Museum
(author memorabilia).

Conn Creek is one of the Napa Valley's easiest-to-find wineries. Located near a well-traveled Rutherford intersection, it occupies a Spanish Mediterranean–style stucco building that blends well with the surroundings.

Conn Creek was founded by Bill Collins, a former submarine officer, and his wife, Kathy. The couple named it for the seasonal tributary of the Napa River that curls behind the present-day tasting room and production facility. The winery quickly won recognition for its wines, notably the 1974 Eisele Vineyard Cabernet Sauvignon. In the mid-1970s, the Collinses took on a partner named Koerner Rombauer.

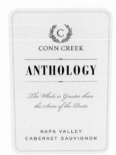

lessons about grape growing and share, using the proceeds to start Collinses continued to farm grapes they sold Conn Creek to its current The legendary André Tchelistcheff, Vineyard and a consultant to Ste. limited-production Bordeaux reds,

Several years later, having absorbed marketing, Rombauer sold his Rombauer Vineyards. Although the for many years, in the mid-1980s owners, Ste. Michelle Wine Estates. the former winemaker at Beaulieu Michelle, participated in a shift to primarily Cabernet Sauvignon.

Bordeaux varietals remain the emphasis, with three distinct portfolios — the Napa Valley Collection, the AVA Series, and the flagship Anthology Bordeaux blend — highlighting various facets of the nation's premier winegrowing region. The Napa Valley Collection focuses on grape types — Cabernet Sauvignon, of course, and also Merlot, Cabernet Franc, and a few others. With the AVA Series, the winery aims to illustrate the diversity of Napa Valley Cabernet Sauvignon through bottlings from Oakville, Diamond Mountain, and several other subappellations. For the Anthology blend, winemaker Elizabeth DeLouise-Gant selects the best AVA Series grapes to create a Cabernet-dominant wine showcasing the Napa Valley as a whole. AVA Series wines are 100 percent Cabernet Sauvignon, but Anthology includes other Bordeaux varietals. At private Anthology Salon tastings, guests can sip Anthology and some Cabernets, in the process learning how the singular soils and climates of the subappellations affect the finished product.

The entertaining and thoughtfully conceived Barrel Blending Experience allows guests to dive even more deeply into the winemaking process, investigating the tastes and textures of hillside versus valley-floor Cabernet Sauvignon, for instance, and of grapes grown in the Napa Valley AVA's cooler versus warmer sections. Participants also examine how in small percentages the other red Bordeaux varietals enhance a wine's aroma, fruitiness, and other attributes. After fashioning a blend, guests bottle, cork, and label their wine, which they can take home as a souvenir.

DOMAINE CARNEROS

DOMAINE CARNEROS
1240 Duhig Rd.
Napa, CA 94559
800-716-BRUT (2788)
707-257-0101
domainecarneros.com

OWNERS: Partnership
between Taittinger and
Kopf families.

LOCATION: Intersection of
Hwys. 121/12 and Duhig
Rd., 4 miles southwest
of the town of Napa and
6 miles southeast of
Sonoma.

APPELLATION: Los Carneros.

HOURS: 10 A.M.–5:30 P.M.
daily.

TASTINGS: $30–$40 for
seated tastings (varies
by tasting selected);
reservations required.

TOURS: 11 A.M., 1 P.M.,
and 3 P.M. daily ($50).

THE WINES: Brut Rosé,
Le Rêve, Pinot Noir,
Vintage Brut.

SPECIALTIES: *Méthode traditionnelle* sparkling wine,
Pinot Noir.

WINEMAKERS: Eileen Crane,
founding winemaker;
TJ Evans and Zak Miller,
winemakers.

ANNUAL PRODUCTION:
48,000 cases.

OF SPECIAL NOTE:
Panoramic views of the
Carneros region. Cheese,
caviar, smoked salmon, and
charcuterie available for
purchase.

NEARBY ATTRACTION:
di Rosa (indoor and
outdoor exhibits of works
by contemporary Bay Area
artists).

An architectural tribute to its French heritage, the impressive Domaine Carneros château is modeled after the home of Champagne Taittinger in Reims, France. Crowning a hillside in the Carneros region of southern Napa, it is situated in a prime growing area for Chardonnay and Pinot Noir, the primary grape varieties used in sparkling wine. A grand staircase framed by fountains and gardens forms the entrance to the winery. French marble floors, high ceilings, and decorative features such as a Louis XV fireplace mantel impart a palatial ambience. Guests can savor a range of sparkling and still wines with local charcuterie, cheese, or caviar while seated at a private table in one of several beautiful locations in the château: the elegant salon, the dramatic glass-enclosed garden conservatory, or the broad, sunny terrace with its panoramic views of rolling Carneros vineyards.

Domaine Carneros started with a quest by the Champagne Taittinger family in Reims, France, for an ideal site in California for growing and producing world-class sparkling wine. They found it in the Carneros, where a long, moderately cool growing season and breezes from San Pablo Bay allow for slow, even ripening; mature flavors; and bright acidity in Pinot Noir and Chardonnay grapes. Established in 1987, Domaine Carneros now includes six certified organic estate vineyards for a total of four hundred acres.

Harvest at Domaine Carneros typically begins in mid-August, when the delicate balance between sugar and acidity is at the optimal point for sparkling wines. Crews head out to pick grapes before dawn, and the fruit is immediately brought to the winery for gentle pressing. Each lot is maintained separately until the perfect blend is determined. At Domaine Carneros, sparkling wines are made in accordance with the rigorous and complex *méthode traditionnelle*, in which secondary fermentation takes place in the bottle. A growing portfolio of fine Pinot Noir still wines has aficionados of the Burgundian varietal praising the winery's production and the expertise of Pinot Noir winemaker TJ Evans.

Heading this multifaceted operation is founding winemaker/CEO Eileen Crane, who has been with Domaine Carneros from the beginning—helping to locate the winery site and develop the vineyards and facilities. Crane is not only one of the industry's pioneering women, but also the most experienced American sparkling winemaker, with more than forty years to her credit, and is widely regarded as the doyenne of sparkling wine in the United States.

FRANK FAMILY VINEYARDS

Frank Family Vineyards' tasting room, one of the most popular destinations in the Napa Valley, was recently redesigned by Erin Martin, whom the *San Francisco Chronicle* calls a "design world supernova." It offers enlivened spaces in which to host tastings: the Patriarch Room, named for Rich Frank's father, a World War II veteran; the Hollywood Room, featuring Rich and Leslie's awards from their Hollywood careers; a gorgeous heated patio with lounge seating and porch swings. The winery introduced The Elevated Experience, an exclusive tasting that pairs limited-production reserve wines with cheese and charcuterie.

Rich, along with his wife, Leslie, an Emmy Award–winning TV journalist, knows how to make visitors feel welcome. The tasting room has been recognized consistently among the best in Napa in Bay Area polls. It has also received critical recognition twice as *Connoisseurs' Guide to California Wine* Winery of the Year and top rankings in the *Wine & Spirits* annual restaurant poll. Visitors taste still and sparkling wines in one of six tasting areas in the yellow Craftsman house. They may also enjoy the grounds, including picnic tables under towering elm trees or rocking chairs on the front porch.

Frank Family is home to a massive stone building constructed in 1884, recorded as the third-oldest winery in Napa. Refurbished in 1906 with local sandstone, it is listed on the National Register of Historic Places and as an official Point of Historical Interest in California.

In 1990 Rich Frank purchased a home and property in Rutherford as a getaway from Hollywood while president of Disney Studios. With a great hillside vineyard, Winston Hill, already in his portfolio, in 1992 he purchased the historic stone winery and in 1993 opened it to the public. He started to build production by acquiring additional vineyards, including Benjamin Vineyard in Rutherford, Lewis Vineyard in the Carneros, and S&J Vineyard in Capell Valley. Today the winery owns nearly four hundred acres of vineyards, which winemaker Todd Graff utilizes to produce Frank's wines. While the winery has been credited with leading the grower-producer sparkling wine movement in California, the focus is on still wines. Driving Frank Family's acclaim are four distinct Cabernets and Cabernet blends: Napa Valley Cabernet, Rutherford Reserve Cabernet, Winston Hill, and Patriarch. The winery also produces very small quantities of vineyard-designate wines. Carneros Chardonnay is Frank Family's most popular bottling in the United States.

FRANK FAMILY VINEYARDS
1091 Larkmead Ln.
Calistoga, CA 94515
800-574-9463
info@frankfamily
vineyards.com
frankfamilyvineyards.com

OWNERS: Rich and Leslie Frank.

LOCATION: About 5 miles north of downtown St. Helena via Hwy. 29.

APPELLATIONS: Chiles Valley, Los Carneros, Napa Valley, Rutherford.

HOURS: 10 A.M.–5 P.M. daily; reservations required Friday–Sunday, recommended Monday–Thursday.

TASTINGS: $40 for sparkling wine and reserve wines; $85 for Elevated Experience of winery-exclusive wines plus artisanal cheeses and charcuterie.

TOURS: None.

THE WINES: Cabernet Sauvignon, Chardonnay, late-harvest Chardonnay, Petite Sirah, Pinot Noir, Port, Sangiovese, Zinfandel.

SPECIALTIES: Cabernet Sauvignon from Rutherford, sparkling wine, Chardonnay from Carneros.

WINEMAKER: Todd Graff.

ANNUAL PRODUCTION: 100,000 cases.

OF SPECIAL NOTE: Picnic tables for use by visitors. *Méthode champenoise* wines and some still wines available only at winery. Two-time *Connoisseurs' Guide to California Wine* Winery of the Year winner; top rankings in *Wine & Spirits* annual restaurant-wines poll.

NEARBY ATTRACTION: Bothe-Napa State Park (hiking, picnicking, horseback riding, swimming).

GOOSECROSS CELLARS

GOOSECROSS CELLARS
1119 State Ln.
Yountville, CA 94599
707-944-1986
wine@goosecross.com
goosecross.com

OWNERS:
Coors family.

LOCATION: 2 miles
northeast of downtown
Yountville off Yountville
Cross Rd.

APPELLATIONS: Atlas Peak,
Calistoga, Howell Moun-
tain, Los Carneros, Oak
Knoll, Oakville, Yountville.

HOURS: 10 A.M.–4:30 P.M.
daily.

TASTINGS: $40 for 5 or
6 wines; $100 for Cabernet
reserve tasting of 5 wines.
Reservations required.

TOURS: By appointment.

THE WINES: Cabernet
Franc, Cabernet Sauvi-
gnon, Chardonnay, Merlot,
Petite Sirah, Pinot Noir,
Sauvignon Blanc, Syrah.

SPECIALTIES: Small-
production single-
vineyard estate-grown
Cabernet Sauvignon, Cab-
ernet Franc, and Merlot.
Branta Syrah-based red
blend; Aeros and other
Bordeaux-style red blends.

WINEMAKER:
Bill Nancarrow.

ANNUAL PRODUCTION:
6,000 cases.

OF SPECIAL NOTE: Patio
located at vineyard's edge.
Events include Burgers
and Branta (mid-August)
and Aeros dinner (early
December). All wines
available only in tasting
room.

NEARBY ATTRACTION: Napa
Valley Wine Museum
(winemaking displays, art
exhibits).

own a placid country lane two miles from downtown Yountville's shops and famous restaurants, Goosecross Cellars hides in nearly plain sight. Established in 1985, this boutique valley-floor winery cultivated a loyal fan base for its easygoing hospitality and diverse lineup—Napa stalwarts like Chardonnay, Sauvignon Blanc, and Cabernet Sauvignon, as well as wines from Pinot Noir, Petite Sirah, and several other varietals.

"We pretty much have something for everyone's palate," says Christi Coors Ficeli, who along with other members of the Coors  brewing family purchased the winery from its founders in 2013. Between marketing and distribution jobs at her family's company, Coors Ficeli learned about the wine business while working for E&J Gallo Winery in Northern California. The newly minted vintner made an instant local splash by hiring Bill Nancarrow, who departed his role as executive winemaker at Duckhorn Vineyards to get his "hands dirty again" at this much smaller operation.

Nancarrow, a New Zealander who made wines in his native land before joining Duckhorn, recalls sensing from the start that Goosecross Cellars was an "unpolished diamond." The "purity and inno-cence" of wines from the estate State Lane Vineyard impressed the winemaker, who saw the potential to further elevate the quality with tweaks to the vineyard and winery practices.

In upgrading the tasting space, Coors Ficeli likewise sought to retain the down-home ambience that has made Goosecross Cellars a favorite of concierges and private tour guides wanting to provide clients with an authentic, off-the-beaten-path Napa Valley outing. Since the debut of a new concrete, steel, and glass production facility in 2015, guests sip wines in a barnlike contemporary tasting room that's more functional than fancy yet stylishly done. The two-story dormered structure looks as if made of board and batten, but is actually concrete stamped to look that way. Retractable rear windows reveal western vistas of State Lane Vineyard, oak-studded Yountville Hill, and, in the distance, the Mayacamas Mountains. When the weather is nice, most visitors head outside to the patio.

The vines nearest the tasting room are part of Holly's Block, named for Coors Ficeli's grand-mother. Grapes from this section go into the Holly's Block Cabernet, the flagship Aeros made from most of the red Bordeaux varietals grown here, and the State Lane Vineyard Cabernet Sauvignon. These three wines plus two others from State Lane—Merlot and Cabernet Franc—are served at special tastings, accompanied by cheese and charcuterie, in a small room off the one where a few years before the wines aged in oak barrels.

GRGICH HILLS ESTATE

F ew people driving along Highway 29 recognize both of the red, white, and blue flags flying in front of this winery. They certainly know one, the American flag. The other represents Croatia, the native country of winemaker and co-owner Miljenko "Mike" Grgich.

The simple red-tile-roofed, white stucco building may not be as flashy as those of nearby wineries, but as the saying goes, it's what's inside that counts. Once visitors pass beneath the grapevine trellis and into the dimly lit recesses of the tasting room, they forget about exterior appearances. The comfortable, old-world atmosphere at Grgich Hills Estate is not a gimmick.

The winery was founded by Miljenko "Mike" Grgich (pronounced "GUR-gitch") and Austin E. Hills on July 4, 1977. Both were already well known. Hills is a member of the Hills Brothers coffee family. Grgich was virtually legendary, especially in France. He had drawn worldwide attention in 1976, when, at the now-famous Paris tasting, an all-French panel of judges chose his 1973 Chateau Montelena Chardonnay over the best of the white Burgun- dies in a blind tasting. It was a momentous occasion for the California wine industry in general and in particular for Mike Grgich, who was already acknowledged as one of the state's top winemakers.

Finally in a position to capitalize on his fame, Grgich quickly found a simpatico partner in Hills, who had a background in business and finance and was the owner of established vineyards. The two men shortly began turning out the intensely flavored Chardonnays that remain the flagship wines of Grgich Hills Estate.

Grgich, easily recognizable with his trademark blue beret, was born in 1923 into a winemaking family on the Dalmatian coast of Croatia. He arrived in California in 1958 and spent his early years at Beaulieu Vineyard, where he worked with the late, pioneering winemaker André Tchelistcheff before moving on to Mondavi and Chateau Montelena. Grgich continues to make wine and relies on a younger generation—daughter Violet Grgich, president, and nephew Ivo Jeramaz, vice president of vineyards and production—to carry on the family tradition. Visitors to Grgich Hills Estate may well run into family members when taking the exceptionally informative winery tour, available twice a day by appointment, or while sampling wines in the cool, cellarlike tasting room or in the VIP tasting room and hospitality center.

GRGICH HILLS ESTATE
1829 St. Helena Hwy.
(Hwy. 29)
Rutherford, CA 94573
800-532-3057
info@grgich.com
grgich.com

OWNERS: Miljenko "Mike" Grgich and Austin Hills.

LOCATION: About 3 miles south of St. Helena.

APPELLATION: Napa Valley.

HOURS: 9:30 A.M.–4:30 P.M. daily.

TASTINGS: $25 for 5 wines.

TOURS: By appointment, 11 A.M. and 2 P.M. daily.

THE WINES: Cabernet Sauvignon, Chardonnay, Fumé Blanc, Merlot, Violetta (late-harvest dessert wine), Zinfandel.

SPECIALTIES: Chardonnay, Cabernet Sauvignon.

WINEMAKER: Mike Grgich.

ANNUAL PRODUCTION: 65,000 cases.

OF SPECIAL NOTE: Behind the scenes tour and tasting by appointment. Grape stomping offered daily during harvest. Napa Valley Wine Train stops at Grgich Hills for special tour and tasting; call 800-427-4124 for schedule. Winery marked 40th anniversary in 2017.

NEARBY ATTRACTIONS: Bothe-Napa State Park (hiking, picnicking, horseback riding, swimming); Bale Grist Mill State Historic Park (waterpowered mill circa 1846); Robert Louis Stevenson Museum (author memorabilia).

THE HESS COLLECTION WINERY

THE HESS COLLECTION WINERY
4411 Redwood Rd.
Napa, CA 94558
707-255-1144
hesscollection.com

FOUNDER: Donald Hess.

LOCATION: 7 miles west of Hwy. 29.

APPELLATIONS: Mt. Veeder, Napa Valley.

HOURS: 10 A.M.–5:30 P.M. daily.

TASTINGS: $25–$100. Various food-and-wine pairings ($35–$185) offered daily by reservation.

TOURS: Art collection open daily; museum admission is free. Guided tours of winery and collection by appointment.

THE WINES: Cabernet Sauvignon, Chardonnay, Malbec, Petite Syrah, Sauvignon Blanc, Viognier, Zinfandel.

SPECIALTIES: Mount Veeder Cabernet Sauvignon, Chardonnay, Malbec.

WINEMAKERS: David Guffy, Randle Johnson, Stephanie Pope.

ANNUAL PRODUCTION: Unavailable.

OF SPECIAL NOTE: Extensive collection of contemporary art. Many wines available only in tasting room.

NEARBY ATTRACTIONS: di Rosa (indoor and outdoor exhibits of works by contemporary Bay Area artists); Alston Regional Park (hiking).

A gently winding road heads up a forested mountainside to this winery on the western rim of the Napa Valley. Although only a fifteen-minute drive from bustling Highway 29, the estate feels a thousand times removed. Arriving visitors are greeted with stunning vineyard views from almost every vantage point.

Swiss entrepreneur Donald Hess has owned vineyards on Mount Veeder since 1978, so when he decided to establish his own winery, he didn't have to look far to find the Christian Brothers Mont La Salle property. He already knew that the east side of the extinct volcano provided a cool climate that allowed a long growing season as well as excellent soil drainage — two viticultural components

known for producing Cabernet ture and superb concentration were first planted on this land in three-story stone winery was built produced wine here for nearly a facilities to Hess in 1986. He began yards on terrain so steep they have must grow extended roots to cling resultant stress creates fruit of exceptional character.

Sauvignon with excellent struc- of aromas and flavors. Vineyards the 1860s, long before the ivy-clad, in 1903. The Christian Brothers half century before leasing the planting Cabernet Sauvignon vine- to be picked by hand. The vines to the mountainside, and the

The Hess Collection farms 310 acres of Mount Veeder vineyards that range in elevation from six hundred to two thousand feet. Viewing itself as a steward of the land, the winery farms these vineyards using the principles of sustainable agriculture. The vineyards and winery have been certified by the Napa Green program of the Napa Valley Vintners.

Hess spent three years renovating the facility before opening it to the public in 1989. The overhaul included transforming 13,000 square feet on the second and third floors to display his extensive collection of international art, which consists of 143 paintings, sculptures, and interactive pieces by modern and contemporary artists, among them such luminaries as Francis Bacon, Frank Stella, Anselm Kiefer, Andy Goldsworthy, and Robert Motherwell. One work evokes a particularly strong response for its social commentary. It is Argentinean Leopold Maler's *Hommage 1974*, an eternally burning typewriter created in protest of the repression of artistic freedom.

The tasting room, which shares the first floor with a century-old barrel-aging cellar, is built from a local iron-rich limestone quarried from the property. The stone had been covered with stucco by the Christian Brothers but was inadvertently exposed during the winery's renovation. This is where visitors linger and share their impressions of both the wine and the art.

LAIRD FAMILY ESTATE

West of Highway 29 between Napa and Yountville, the patinated-copper roof of the Laird Family Estate tasting space points discreetly skyward, glowing a subtle green throughout the grape-growing season amid the 185 verdant acres of Chardonnay and Cabernet Sauvignon vines that surround it. Like many of the winery's initiatives, the concrete-and-glass structure, completed in 1999, involves a well-executed deal by founders Ken and Gail Laird.

Three decades earlier, Laird, an engineer by trade with a desire to break into the wine-grape business, spotted a Calistoga prune orchard he thought suitable for a vineyard. Arranging financing, however, proved more difficult than Laird imagined: a local bank turned him down because he hadn't secured contracts with wineries to purchase the grapes. With characteristic aplomb, he went straight to the top, seeking advice from famed vintner Robert Mondavi, who told him what to plant and agreed to buy the crop long term. Mondavi's commitment in hand, Laird re-ceived his loan. The Calistoga site, since sold, was the first of many real estate transactions. With 40 properties and more than 2,200 acres under vine, Laird's company ranks as the Napa Valley's largest vineyard business. Laird sold fruit for many years and later opened custom-crush facilities where other wineries could produce wines. Starting in 1999, bottles bearing his name debuted.

Ken and Gail's son Justin Laird supervises the vineyard operations these days, while daughter Rebecca Laird manages the custom-crush facilities and tasting room. About 97 percent of the grapes go to customers that include Mumm Napa, Nickel & Nickel, and Cakebread Cellars, with 3 percent held back for the dozen-plus small-lot wines crafted by winemaker Brian Mox. Laird is known for Chardonnay and Cabernet Sauvignon and also makes two Los Carneros Pinot Noirs, one from the appellation's most southern tip and the other from the eastern region. All the Laird wines except for one blend are single varietal. The exception, Jillian's Blend, named for Ken and Gail's granddaughter, is the winery's top seller. Its largest component is Cabernet Sauvignon, but Mox adds texture and layers of flavor with Syrah, Merlot, Malbec, and Petit Verdot.

Tastings at Laird are casual. Wide windows and a vaulted ceiling punctuated by frosted pendant lights created by a local jeweler lend an airy feel to the main tasting space. In good weather, guests sip alfresco on an Ipe-wood terrace that has Mount Veeder views in the distance and up-close ones of four stainless-steel chutes. Much of the year they gleam dormant in the sun, but at harvesttime truck after truck off-loads grapes down them, the hustle and bustle a tribute to Ken Laird's determination and ingenuity.

LAIRD FAMILY ESTATE
5055 Solano Ave.
Napa, CA 94558
707-257-0360, ext. 26
877-297-4902, ext. 26
info@lairdfamilyestate.com
lairdfamilyestate.com

OWNERS: Ken and Gail Laird.

LOCATION: 5 miles north of downtown Napa via Hwy. 29.

APPELLATION: Oak Knoll District of Napa Valley.

HOURS: 10 A.M.–5 P.M. daily.

TASTINGS: $20 for Standard Tasting of 5 wines; $30 for Reds Only Tasting of 5 wines. Reservations required for a party of 6 or more.

TOURS: Available with 24-hour notice, except on weekends, no charge.

THE WINES: Cabernet Sauvignon, Chardonnay, Malbec, Pinot Grigio, Pinot Noir, Sauvignon Blanc, Syrah.

SPECIALTIES: Brut Sparkling Rosé, Cold Creek Ranch Chardonnay, Flat Rock Ranch and Mast Ranch Yountville Cabernet Sauvignons, Jillian's Blend, proprietary red blends.

WINEMAKER: Brian Mox.

ANNUAL PRODUCTION: 15,000 cases.

OF SPECIAL NOTE: Tree-shaded picnic area (no food sold on-site). Winery is family friendly and pet friendly; picnickers are welcome. Brut Rosé, Malbec, and Syrah available only in tasting room.

NEARBY ATTRACTION: CIA at Copia (wine and culinary exhibitions; cooking demonstrations).

MADRIGAL FAMILY WINERY

MADRIGAL FAMILY WINERY
3718 N. St. Helena Hwy.
(Hwy. 29)
Calistoga, CA 94515
707-942-8619
tastingroom@
madrigalfamilywinery.com
madrigalfamilywinery.com

OWNER: Chris Madrigal.

LOCATION: St. Helena Hwy.,
.25 mile south of Larkmead
Ln.

APPELLATIONS: Calistoga,
Napa Valley.

HOURS: Daily, by
appointment.

TASTINGS: $35 for Madrigal
Family Tasting of 5 wines;
$50 for Reserve Tasting of
5 wines.

TOURS: By request.

THE WINES: Cabernet Franc,
Cabernet Sauvignon, Fumé
Blanc, Gewürztraminer,
Grenache, Petit Verdot,
Petite Sirah, Port, Rosé,
Tempranillo, Zinfandel.

SPECIALTIES: Small-lot estate-
grown wines, including
Cabernet Sauvignon and
Petite Sirah; Fumé Blanc;
Petite Sirah Port; Rosé of
Grenache.

WINEMAKER: Chris Madrigal.

ANNUAL PRODUCTION:
10,000 cases.

OF SPECIAL NOTE: Artisan
cheese pairing and lunch
available with 72-hour and
24-hour notice, respectively.
Most wines sold only in
tasting rooms. Second
tasting room located at 819
Bridgeway, Sausalito, and
open daily 12–7 P.M.

NEARBY ATTRACTIONS:
Bothe-Napa Valley State
Park (hiking, picnicking,
horseback riding,
swimming); Culinary
Institute of America
at Greystone (cooking
demonstrations); Bale Grist
Mill State Park (water-
powered mill circa 1846).

The hacienda-like Madrigal Family Winery building sits east of St. Helena Highway amid a swath of southern Calistoga rich with history. Like most Napa wineries, this small operation that produced its first vintage in 1995 makes Cabernet Sauvignon. Petite Sirah was another early claim to fame, but with nearly a dozen other wines, including Gewürztraminer, Cabernet Franc, Garnacha (Grenache), and Tempranillo, Madrigal provides wine lovers the opportunity to expand their palates at unpretentious tastings that often take place outdoors.

"This is what Napa Valley was like thirty years ago," says owner-winemaker Chris Madrigal, and he should know: his family his grandfather, Jacinto Madrigal, Napa Valley. From what Chris an ironwood tasting platform that vineyard, he can gaze east across Vineyards (now Davis Estates),

has been here since 1938, when emigrated from Mexico to the describes as his "infinity deck," juts into Madrigal's forty-acre estate the valley to the former Saviez where Jacinto tended the vines.

Decades later, when Chris and their vineyard-management com-fields. Their big break came in 1986 his father, Jess, were establishing pany, they, too, farmed the Saviez when Clos Pegase Winery hired them on a few days' notice. "At the time, all we owned were pruning shears and a pickup truck," recalls Chris. With pruning and tilling set to commence, father and son scrambled to acquire the necessary equipment. The Clos Pegase gig led to one with Duckhorn Vineyards, now famous but then a mere decade old. Among Jess and Chris's early Duckhorn projects was redeveloping the legendary Three Palms Vineyard. Chris purchased his vineyard from the Duckhorns to start Madrigal Family Winery. In the nineteenth century, Three Palms, the Madrigal property, other nearby vineyards, and much of what is now Bothe-Napa Valley State Park were part of the estate of Charles and Martha Hitchcock. Their daughter, Lillie Hitchcock Coit — San Francisco's Coit Tower is named for her — developed several nearby vineyards, among them Three Palms.

Chris appreciates his family's place in Calistoga history. Present-day Napa Valley, awash with big money and fancy architecture, sometimes seems adrift from its agricultural roots, but Chris strives to keep alive the spirit of grit, cooperation, and relaxed hospitality he believes helped the region attain international prominence. "We're a true family winery, old school," says Chris. When people visit, he adds, "We want them to be sold on the wine, but also us." The many repeat guests, some of whom first learn about the winery by happening upon its second tasting room in downtown Sausalito in Marin County, are among the clues that Chris and his team succeed on both counts.

MATERRA|CUNAT FAMILY VINEYARDS

MATERRA|CUNAT FAMILY VINEYARDS
4326 Big Ranch Rd.
Napa, CA 94558
707-224-4900
info@materrawines.com
materrawines.com

OWNERS: Brian and
John Cunat.

LOCATION: 1.3 miles east of
Hwy. 29 and .9 mile west
of Silverado Trail.

APPELLATIONS: Oak Knoll
District of Napa Valley,
Howell Mountain, Diamond
Mountain District, Calistoga,
St. Helena, Rutherford.

HOURS: 10 A.M.–4 P.M. daily,
by appointment.

TASTINGS: $25 for 5 or 6
wines. $50 for reserve tasting
of 5 or 6 wines (48-hour
advance notice required).

TOURS: 11 A.M.–3 P.M. daily,
by appointment.

THE WINES: Cabernet Sauvignon, Chardonnay, Merlot,
Midnight (red blend of
predominantly Petit Verdot
and Malbec), Petite Sirah,
Sauvignon Blanc, Syrah,
Viognier.

SPECIALTY: Merlot-based
blends.

CONSULTING WINEMAKERS:
Bruce Regalia and Michael
Trujillo.

ANNUAL PRODUCTION:
6,000–7,000 cases.

OF SPECIAL NOTE: Historic
site. Winery is pet friendly.
Interactive demonstration
vineyards. Occasional
educational tours and
tastings. Japanese-style
bidets in restrooms. Gallery
with rotating exhibits, small
gift shop, library room for
reserve tasting.

NEARBY ATTRACTION: Napa
Valley Museum (winemak-
ing displays, art exhibits).

Brian Cunat grew up on a farm in Illinois, where he developed a strong work ethic and a deep respect for farming and agriculture. While building a successful international real estate business and serving as the youngest president of Kiwanis International, he and his wife, Miki, a native of Japan, traveled the world. Along the way, they toured wineries, ambled through vineyards, and developed a passion for international cuisine paired with world-class wines. In 2007 Cunat decided to combine his love of wine and his farming experience by purchasing a fifty-acre property in the Oak Knoll District of Napa Valley, where Chardonnay vines had flourished for more than a century. He named it Cunat Family Vineyards, gathered an expert team of vineyard managers and winemakers, and planted Merlot, Petit Verdot, Malbec, Chardonnay, Sauvignon Blanc, and Viognier vines with the aim of producing exceptional fruit to transform into first-rate wines.

Cunat also built a cutting-edge winery that opened in 2015. Coined from two Latin words, *mater* (mother) and *terra* (earth), the name reflects the family's commitment to nurturing Mother Earth's gifts of sun, soil, water, and all the elements that contribute to a successful growing season. The vineyards are mostly dry-farmed using environmentally sustainable methods. The facility features state-of-the-art equipment and embraces the very latest technology for production, storage, and hospitality, designed to produce little to no waste and the least possible impact on the planet.

Members of the Cunat family are involved in all facets of the business. Brian and Miki's daughter, Neena, oversaw daily operations for seven years. Her younger sister, Amie, designed the wine labels and interior decoration. Brian's brother, John, and the extended Cunat family are supportive investors. The family participates actively in the winemaking process, guided by well-known consulting winemakers Bruce Regalia and Michael Trujillo, each with more than thirty years in the business. Regalia's experience includes winemaking duties at Duckhorn Wine Company and Goldeneye in Anderson Valley. Trujillo learned alongside legendary winemakers André Tchelistcheff, Tony Soter, and Jim Allen and currently directs the wine program at Sequoia Grove Winery in Napa.

The minimalist interior, with stainless-steel embellishments and polished concrete floors, is designed to encourage a focus on the wines. Elegant sit-down tastings are conducted at rustic hemlock tables in a private tasting room or at picnic tables on the spacious outdoor patio surrounded by panoramic views of the Mayacamas and Vaca mountains. Native and drought-tolerant landscaping graces the exterior.

MUMM NAPA

MUMM NAPA
8445 Silverado Trail
Rutherford, CA 94573
707-967-7700
mumm_info@mumm
napa.com
mummnapa.com

OWNER: Pernod Ricard USA.

LOCATION: East of
Rutherford, 1 mile south
of Rutherford Cross Rd.

APPELLATION: Napa Valley.

HOURS: 10 A.M.–6 P.M. daily
(last seating at 5:45 P.M.).

TASTINGS: $25 and up for
flights, $12 and up by the
flute, $45 and up for Oak
Terrace tasting.

TOURS: 10 A.M., 11 A.M.,
1 P.M., and 3 P.M. daily.

THE WINES: Blanc de
Blancs, Blanc de Noirs,
Brut Prestige, Brut Reserve,
Brut Rosé, Demi-Sec, DVX,
Sparkling Pinot Noir.

SPECIALTIES: Sparkling wine
made in traditional French
style; Devaux Ranch single-
vineyard estate sparkling
wine.

WINEMAKER:
Ludovic Dervin.

ANNUAL PRODUCTION:
450,000 cases.

OF SPECIAL NOTE: Collection
of Ansel Adams photography
and exhibitions of works by
renowned photographers
(free admission). Majority
of wines available only at
winery. Limited availability
of large-format bottles at
winery.

NEARBY ATTRACTION:
Napa Valley Museum
(winemaking displays,
art exhibits).

For connoisseurs of Champagne, relaxing outdoors on a sunny day with a glass of bubbly, in the company of good friends, taking in a panoramic vineyard view, may be the ultimate pleasure. This is obviously what Champagne Mumm of France had in mind when in 1979 it dispatched the late Guy Devaux to North America to establish a winery that could develop a sparkling wine that would live up to Champagne standards.

Devaux, a native of Epernay, the epicenter of France's Champagne district, was an expert on *méthode champenoise.* In

this French style of wine-making, the wine under-goes its bubble-producing fermentation in the very bottle from which it will be poured. After crisscrossing the United States for four years conducting research, Devaux decreed the Napa Valley, with its varied soils and hot summer days and cool evenings and early mornings, the locale most capable of producing grapes with the acidity required of distinguished sparkling wines.

As founding winemaker, Devaux established the house style of blending wines from numerous sources, and his current successor, Ludovic Dervin, continues the tradition. Mumm Napa prides itself on its relationships with more than fifty noteworthy growers, some of whom have been farming for five generations. Dervin, a Champagne native with experience at wineries in both France and California, blends wines made from individual grape lots to create widely distributed offerings such as Mumm Napa's signature Brut Prestige and rarer ones that include the vintage-dated series DVX—Devaux's name minus the vowels. Mumm Napa also honored Devaux by naming its sole single-vineyard bottling, Devaux Ranch, after him, along with the Carneros site where the wine's Chardonnay, Pinot Noir, and Pinot Meunier grapes are grown.

DVX wines—equal parts Chardonnay and Pinot Noir—are featured along with reserve wines in seated Oak Terrace tastings, shaded by large umbrellas and the outstretched branches of a nearly two-century-old blue oak tree. A plate of cheeses, nuts, and fresh and dried fruit accompanies the wines. Flights and wines by the glass are poured in the light-filled salon and on the adjoining open-air patio. Mumm Napa's tours cover the sparkling winemaking process, including grape varietals and vineyard management, fermentation, blending, bottling, aging, and *dosage,* the process of adding wine mixed with pure sugar to create the requisite residual sugar level for the type of wine (drier or sweeter) being made. Tours conclude at the photography gallery, which displays twenty-seven original Ansel Adams prints and presents exhibitions of other well-regarded photographers' works.

PEJU

Spotting Peju, even on a winery-lined stretch of Highway 29, is easy, thanks to a fifty-foot-tall tasting tower topped with a distinctive copper roof. The tasting tower, like the rest of the property, looks as if it could have been transplanted directly from the countryside of southern France.

The Rutherford estate had been producing wine grapes for more than eighty years when Anthony and Herta Peju bought it in 1983. The couple has been improving the thirty-acre property ever since, honing vineyard techniques and adding Merlot and Cabernet Franc grapes to the estate's core product, Cabernet Sauvignon. By the mid-1990s, demand for Peju wines outstripped the winery's supply. To satisfy it, the Pejus acquired a 350-acre property in northern Napa County in Pope Valley, planted a variety of grapes, and named it Persephone Vineyard, after a goddess in Greek mythology.

Anthony Peju had been living in Europe when he was lured by the movie industry to Los Angeles, where he met Herta Behensky, his future wife. Peju established his own nursery, but had long dreamed of owning a farm. The vibrant towns in Napa Valley and their proximity to San Francisco motivated him to begin a search for vineyard property that ended two years later with the acquisition of what would become Peju Province Winery.

Peju's horticultural experience, combined with his wife's talent for gardening, resulted in two acres of immaculately kept winery gardens. Together, they established a dramatic series of outdoor rooms linked by footpaths and punctuated with fountains and marble sculpture. Hundreds of flowering plants and trees create an aromatic retreat for the Pejus and their visitors. Lining both sides of the driveway are forty-foot-tall sycamore trees, their trunks adorned by gnarled spirals. Visitors reach the tasting room by crossing a small bridge over a pool with fountains. An entrance door of Brazilian cherrywood opens onto a naturally lighted room where three muses grace a century-old stained-glass window.

Celebrating thirty-five years, Peju remains a small, family-owned winery with two generations working together. Since 2001, elder daughter Lisa has traveled the world representing Peju wines and reaching out to younger customers. Ariana, who joined the team in 2006, has spearheaded such environmental initiatives as installing enough solar panels to provide 40 percent of the energy for the winery (now a Napa Green Certified Winery), earning organic certification at Peju's Rutherford estate, and practicing sustainable farming at the winery's other three properties.

PEJU
8466 St. Helena Hwy.
(Hwy. 29)
Rutherford, CA 94573
707-963-3600
info@peju.com
peju.com

OWNERS: Peju family.

LOCATION: 11 miles north of the town of Napa.

APPELLATIONS: Rutherford, Napa Valley.

HOURS: 10 A.M.–6 P.M. daily.

TASTINGS: $25–$150 for Classic Tasting; $75 for Reserve Tasting.

TOURS: Self-guided or by appointment.

THE WINES: Cabernet Franc, Cabernet Sauvignon, Chardonnay, Merlot, Petit Verdot, Province (red and white blend), Rosé, Sauvignon Blanc.

SPECIALTIES: Reserve Cabernet Sauvignon, Reserve Cabernet Franc, The Experiment, Fifty/Fifty, Sketches, H.B. Reserve.

WINEMAKER: Sara Fowler.

ANNUAL PRODUCTION: 35,000 cases.

OF SPECIAL NOTE: Wine-and-food pairings, cooking classes, gift boutique. Barrel tasting by reservation. Art gallery featuring work by contemporary artists. Most wines available only at winery.

NEARBY ATTRACTIONS: Robert Louis Stevenson Museum; Napa Valley Museum (winemaking displays, art exhibits); Culinary Institute of America at Greystone (cooking demonstrations).

THE PRISONER WINE COMPANY

THE PRISONER WINE COMPANY
1178 Galleron Rd.
St. Helena, CA 94574
707-967-3823
877-283-5934
ask@theprisonerwinecompany.com
theprisonerwinecompany.com

OWNER: Constellation Brands.

LOCATION: 3 miles south of downtown St. Helena.

APPELLATIONS: California, Napa Valley.

HOURS: 11 A.M.–6 P.M. daily.

TASTINGS: Line-Up; The Makery: Journey; The Makery: Experience, a wine-and-food pairing. Call for pricing.

TOURS: Some tastings include a tour.

THE WINES: Cabernet Sauvignon, Charbono, Chardonnay, Chenin Blanc, Merlot, Zinfandel.

SPECIALTIES: The Prisoner Napa Valley Red Wine, Blindfold California White Wine, cuttings Cabernet Sauvignon, Saldo Zinfandel.

WINEMAKER: Chrissy Wittmann.

ANNUAL PRODUCTION: 260,000 cases.

OF SPECIAL NOTE: The Makery offers the opportunity to explore the crafts of local Makers, by appointment only. Many wines available only in tasting room.

NEARBY ATTRACTIONS: Bothe-Napa State Park (hiking, picnicking, horseback riding, swimming); Culinary Institute of America at Greystone (cooking demonstrations).

The Prisoner Wine Company struck gold overturning winemaking and marketing conventions. Its flagship wine, The Prisoner, captured attention for its name, edgy label featuring a Francisco de Goya etching of a shackled male, and unusual combination of Zinfandel, Cabernet Sauvignon, Petite Sirah, Syrah, and Charbono grapes. Only a few hundred cases were produced for the debut 2000 vintage, but the wine quickly developed a cult following. Lauded by wine critics as "delicious" and "lush," The Prisoner landed three times on *Wine Spectator* magazine's annual Top 100 Wines list.

Starting in 2016, the company promoted The Prisoner through clever events, one of which brought together artists, designers, and other creators in pop-up "maker" gatherings across the country. When in 2018 the company opened the tasting space in St. Helena, creativity remained a theme. Four studios, called The Makery, feature local artists who draw inspiration from The Prisoner's wines to create unique items. Guests can reserve two distinct private tastings in The Makery. With each season, the programming offers different wines, food pairings, and artistic collaborations.

The Makery is off the Tasting Lounge, which guests enter underneath a hundred-foot-long canopy fashioned out of Teflon. An artwork itself, it's a visual cue that the experience here will shatter a few norms. Inside, Richard Von Saal, a multitalented Napa-based designer, builder, and furniture maker, created a theatrical space whose black, gray, and red color scheme echoes that of The Prisoner label. The feel is almost nightclubby except for the light pouring in through the clerestory window. The overall design doesn't play up the "prison/prisoner" connection overly much, with the striking shackle-like wine rack in the Tasting Lounge being among the few exceptions. Another is, at least in name, the Yard, an outdoor space with a retractable shade system. On some days, chefs working at the smaller kitchen here prepare flatbreads and other dishes.

The culinary emphasis, says executive chef Brett Young, is on bold flavors that showcase the versatility of the company's portfolio. As with The Prisoner, most of the wines are unorthodox blends, such as Blindfold (Chardonnay plus three white Rhône varietals) and Dérangé, which winemaker Chrissy Wittmann describes as "an upside-down version of The Prisoner" with more Cabernet than Zinfandel. She views everyone from industry stalwarts to "mom-and-pop farmers" growing old-vine Zinfandel as collaborators whose artistry in the field and zeal for excellence helped make The Prisoner one of the country's most popular luxury red blends.

QUIXOTE WINERY

Ringed by olive trees and nestled near the rim of a bowl-shaped valley beneath the Stags Leap Palisades, Quixote Winery's production facility and tasting space rank among the Napa Valley's most architecturally significant structures. The only US project of the late Vienna-born artist, architect, philosopher, and environmentalist Friedensreich Hundertwasser, the one-story winery strikes a playful pose with its colorful ceramic tiles and shimmering gold onion dome. Like the sod roof from which it rises, the dome is among the iconoclastic architect's trademarks, as are the curving walls and undulating roofline.

Quixote specializes in estate-grown Stags Leap District Cabernet Sauvignon and Petite Sirah, crafted since 2016 in the silky, elegant style of winemaker Philippe Melka. The highly re-

garded consultant was attracted [...] by Quixote's singular fifty-acre site, bordered by Shafer Vine- [...] yards, whose vines to the north supply grapes for its coveted [...] Hillside Select Cabernet. Melka arrived shortly after new owners [...] purchased Quixote from Carl Doumani, its founder. Doumani, [...] who revived Stags' Leap Winery in the 1970s, retained a small [...] parcel to start Quixote when he sold Stags' Leap to Beringer in [...] 1997. In addition to Cabernet and Petite Sirah, less than an [...] acre of Malbec is planted, along with a few blocks of Cabernet Franc and Petit Verdot.

For much of Doumani's tenure, Aaron Pott, himself a consultant of note, made Quixote's wines. Both Pott and Melka are known for attention to viticultural detail, so these vines, most of them planted in 2002 and farmed organically, have been well tended their entire lives. Although only twenty-seven acres, Quixote's vineyard contains four distinct soil types that, says estate winemaker B.R. Smith, add complexity to the wines, which age nearly two years in French oak barrels and an additional year in bottle. Smooth and drinkable upon release, they can be held for two decades or more.

All tastings at Quixote begin with a brief tour that takes in the vineyard and cellar, with Smith often on hand to describe the grape growing and winemaking. Both Hundertwasser and Doumani, who commissioned the architect's design, were larger-than-life characters, so the hosts have no shortage of anecdotes to draw upon. The leisurely tastings conclude in one of two light-filled spaces. The combination of aesthetic delights and natural beauty—an oval room faces the palisades, and the circular one under the dome has views across the Napa Valley to Mount Veeder—perfectly complements the refined wines Melka composes for this unique hideaway.

QUIXOTE WINERY
6126 Silverado Trail
Napa, CA 94558
707-944-2659
info@quixotewinery.com
quixotewinery.com

OWNER: Quixote LLC.

LOCATION: 7 miles north of downtown Napa.

APPELLATION: Stags Leap District.

HOURS: 10 A.M.–5 P.M. daily.

TASTINGS: $45 for Red Label Experience of 4 wines; $65 for White Label Experience of 5 wines including a reserve selection; $125 for Black Label Experience of 5 wines including a reserve selection. Gourmet cheese plate with Red and White Label tastings, seasonal small bites with Black Label tasting. Reservations required.

TOURS: Tastings include vineyard and winery tour.

THE WINES: Cabernet Sauvignon, Malbec, Petite Sirah.

SPECIALTIES: Single-vineyard estate-grown Cabernet Sauvignon and Petite Sirah; Black Label Cabernet Sauvignon; Block 12 Petite Sirah.

WINEMAKERS: Philippe Melka, consulting winemaker; B. R. Smith, estate winemaker.

ANNUAL PRODUCTION: Unavailable.

OF SPECIAL NOTE: Winery building is architect Friedensreich Hundertwasser's lone US project. Most wines available only in tasting room.

NEARBY ATTRACTIONS: CIA at Copia (cooking demonstrations, food and wine exhibits); Napa Valley Museum (winemaking displays, art exhibits).

ROBERT MONDAVI WINERY

ROBERT MONDAVI WINERY
7801 St. Helena Hwy.
(Hwy. 29)
Oakville, CA 94562
707-968-2001
888-766-6328, option 2
reservations@
robertmondaviwinery.com
robertmondaviwinery.com

LOCATION: About 10 miles
north of the town of Napa.

APPELLATIONS: Oakville,
Napa Valley.

HOURS: 10 A.M.–4:45 P.M.
daily.

TASTINGS: $25–$40 for
4 wines in main tasting
room; $50 for 4 wines or by
the glass in To Kalon Reserve
tasting room.

TOURS: Signature Tour and
Tasting, including To Kalon
Vineyard, by reservation
($40); other tours available
seasonally. Foreign-language
tours by appointment.

THE WINES: Cabernet
Sauvignon, Chardonnay,
Fumé Blanc, I Block Fumé
Blanc, Merlot, Moscato
D'Oro, Pinot Noir, To Kalon
Cabernet Sauvignon.

SPECIALTIES: Cabernet
Sauvignon Reserve and
Fumé Blanc Reserve.

WINEMAKER:
Geneviève Janssens.

ANNUAL PRODUCTION:
200,000 cases.

OF SPECIAL NOTE: Private
cellar tasting and 4-course
wine-pairing dinner
available with advance
reservations. Large retail
shop with wine books
and Italian imports; open
10 A.M.–6 P.M. daily. Summer
Festival Concert Series
(July); Cabernet Sauvignon
Reserve Release Party
(September).

NEARBY ATTRACTIONS:
Culinary Institute of
America at Greystone
(cooking demonstrations);
Napa Valley Museum.

Wineries come and wineries go in Napa Valley, but in this fast-paced, high-stakes world, few can challenge the lasting achievements of the Robert Mondavi Winery. Since its inception more than forty years ago, it has remained in the forefront of innovation, from the use of cold fermentation, stainless-steel tanks, and small French oak barrels to the collaboration with NASA employing aerial imaging to reveal the health and vigor of grapevines.

Founder Robert Mondavi's cherished goal of producing wines on a par with the best in the world made his name virtually synonymous with California winemaking. That vision is being carried out today with ambitious programs such as the To Kalon Project. Named after the historic estate vineyard surrounding the winery, this extensive renovation led to the unveiling of the To Kalon Fermentation Cellar, which capitalizes on the natural flow of gravity to transport wine through the production system. Prized for their ability to enhance aromas, flavors, and complexity in red wines, the cellar's fifty-six French oak fermenting tanks were hand-crafted in Cognac by the renowned cooperage Taransaud. Coopers

numbered each stave before disassembling the fermenters for shipping to Oakville, where the team reconstructed them in place at the winery.

Technological advances aside, the best reason for visiting Robert Mondavi Winery is something less tangible: an opportunity to experience the presentation of wine in the broader context of lifestyle. Educational tours and tastings, concerts, art exhibits, and the industry's first culinary programs are all part of the Mondavi legacy. One of the most popular offerings is the Signature Tour and Tasting, which follows the path of the grape from the vine through the cellar to the finished wine. The 550-acre vineyard was named To Kalon (Greek for "the beautiful") by Hamilton Walker Crabb, a winegrowing pioneer who established vineyards here in the late 1800s. It was this property that inspired Robert Mondavi to establish his winery on the site.

The winery's Spanish mission-style architecture, with its expansive archway and bell tower designed by Clifford May, pays homage to the Franciscan fathers who planted the first grapes in the region. Two long wings project from the open-air lobby to embrace a wide expanse of lawn framed by the Mayacamas Mountains on the western horizon. Typical of the winery's commitment to the arts, several sculptures by regional artist Beniamino Benvenuto Bufano (who, like Robert Mondavi's family, came from Italy) are displayed in the courtyard and elsewhere around the grounds. In addition, the winery features art exhibits that change every two months.

ROMBAUER VINEYARDS

The quarter-mile-long drive from the Silverado Trail leads to a winery ensconced in a forest of pine trees. On the far side of the low-slung building, a wide California ranch–style porch affords views that extend to the tree-covered ridge of the Mayacamas Mountains to the west. Without another structure in sight, the serene setting has the ambience of a fairy-tale kingdom secluded from the hustle and bustle of the valley floor. Directly below the winery, a garden path winds down to a hill where roses are planted in the sun and azaleas thrive in the shade. Scattered about are a half-dozen metal sculptures of fantastical creatures such as a diminutive dinosaur and a life-size winged horse, all weathered to the point that they blend into the landscape.

The Rombauer family traces its heritage to another fertile wine area, the Rheingau region in Germany, where Koerner Rombauer's ancestors made wine. His great-aunt Irma Rombauer wrote the classic book *The Joy of Cooking*. The tradition of linking wine to food is carried on today, with members of the family involved in the operations of the winery, from selecting grapes to marketing the final product.

Koerner Rombauer, a former commercial airline captain, and his wife, Joan, met and married in Southern California, where both had grown up in an agricultural environment. Since they had always wanted their children to have rural childhood experiences similar to their own, they came to the Napa Valley in search of land. In 1972 they bought fifty acres and settled into a home just up the hill from where the winery sits today. Within a few years, they became partners in a nearby winery. Their hands-on involvement in the winery's operations whetted their appetite for a label of their own and for making handcrafted wines with the passion and commitment of the family tradition. Taking advantage of the topography, the Rombauers built their family winery into the side of the hill. Rombauer Vineyards was completed in 1982.

By the early 1990s, the Rombauers realized they had the perfect location for excavating wine storage caves. Completed in 1997, the double-horseshoe-shaped cellar extends for more than a mile into the hillside. When visitors enter the tasting room, they find a personalized space with an eclectic assortment of memorabilia from Koerner Rombauer's life. Guests may also get an occasional glimpse of another of Koerner's passions—one of the automobiles from his private collection of vintage cars.

ROMBAUER VINEYARDS
3522 Silverado Trail North
St. Helena, CA 94574
800-622-2206
707-963-5170
rombauer.com

OWNERS:
Rombauer family.

LOCATION: 1.5 miles north of Deer Park Rd.

APPELLATION: Napa Valley.

HOURS: 10 A.M.–5 P.M. daily.

TASTINGS: $25, by appointment.

TOURS: Cave tours by appointment.

THE WINES: Cabernet Sauvignon, Chardonnay, Merlot, Sauvignon Blanc, Zinfandel.

SPECIALTIES: Limited-production and single-vineyard Cabernet Sauvignon, Zinfandel, and Chardonnay; Best of the Cellar Bordeaux blend; dessert wines.

WINEMAKER: Richie Allen.

ANNUAL PRODUCTION: 225,000 cases.

OF SPECIAL NOTE: Copies of the latest edition of *The Joy of Cooking* and other cookbooks by Irma Rombauer are available in the tasting room. Zinfandel Port and Joy, a late-harvest Chardonnay, available only at winery.

NEARBY ATTRACTIONS: Culinary Institute of America at Greystone (cooking demonstrations); Bothe-Napa State Park (hiking, picnicking, horseback riding, swimming); Robert Louis Stevenson Museum (author memorabilia).

SILVERADO VINEYARDS

SILVERADO VINEYARDS
6121 Silverado Trail
Napa, CA 94558
707-257-1770
info@silveradovineyards
.com
silveradovineyards.com

OWNERS: Ron Miller
and family.

LOCATION: About 2 miles
east of Yountville.

APPELLATIONS: Coombsville,
Los Carneros, Napa
Valley, Stags Leap District,
Yountville.

HOURS: 10 A.M.–5 P.M. daily

TASTINGS: $40 for 4 wines;
$45 for premier flight of 4
red wines. $50 for Terrace
Table Side Service, reserved
table and flight of 4 wines.
$60 Library Tasting of
4 Cabernet Sauvignons
from each decade since
Silverado's inception (fee
varies), by appointment.

TOURS: Guided tour and
tasting, $60, Monday–
Friday, 10:30 a.m. and
2:30 p.m. Vineyard
Tour, $100 per person
(two-person minimum),
by appointment,
May–October. Seasonal
appetizers included.

THE WINES: Cabernet Franc,
Cabernet Sauvignon,
Chardonnay, Late Harvest
Sémillon, Malbec, Merlot,
Petit Verdot, Rosato di
Sangiovese, Sangiovese,
Sauvignon Blanc, Zinfandel.

SPECIALTIES: SOLO Stags
Leap District Cabernet
Sauvignon, GEO
Coombsville Cabernet
Sauvignon.

WINEMAKER:
Jonathan Emmerich.

ANNUAL PRODUCTION:
68,000 cases.

OF SPECIAL NOTE: Historic
art collection on display by
private tour. Many wines
available only in tasting room.

In 1880 famed author Robert Louis Stevenson lived in a shack in an abandoned mining town called Silverado, on the slopes of Mount St. Helena, at the northern end of the Napa Valley. He published reflections of his wine country experience in a book, *The Silverado Squatters*, in which he wrote: "The beginning of vine planting is like the beginning of mining for the precious metals: the wine-grower also 'prospects.'"

Stevenson's statement rang true for Lilian Disney and for Diane Disney Miller and her husband, Ron. Enthused by the wines coming from Napa Valley and captivated by the valley's beauty, they purchased two neighboring vineyards in the mid-1970s and began to "prospect." The Millers initially sold their grapes to local vintners, who made gold medal–winning wines from them. Inspired by this success, they established Silverado Vineyards in 1981 and started construction on a 30,000-square-foot winery. The winery opened to the public six years later. The Millers named the winery after the historic name of the vineyard, which was its new home.

Today Silverado Vine-yards farms 350 acres on six Napa Valley vineyards. Five were first planted by Napa winegrowing pioneers between 1865 and 1895. Each ranch played an important role in establishing the reputation of its growing area. Winemaker Jon Emmerich has made Silverado's estate and single-vineyard wines since 1998, specializing in Cabernet Sauvignon. Most wines express the historic character and flavors of the particular vineyard site. In 1999 UC Davis granted heritage status to the Silverado clone of Cabernet; it is one of only three Cabernet Sauvignon clones to achieve this distinction and the only one from the Stags Leap District. Silverado's flagship SOLO wine is crafted exclusively from its heritage clone, while the GEO wine showcases the bounty of its historic Mount George vineyard.

Guests sample the wines at the Silverado Vineyards estate, where three generations of Millers are still "prospecting" for wine. A steep, curving driveway leads to the spectacular two-story visitor center, a vision in ocher and terra-cotta, stone and stucco, that brings Tuscany to mind. Huge antique beams of Douglas fir span the ceiling. French doors offer stunning north-facing panoramas of vineyards and the hilly Stags Leap landscape. Guests are welcome to explore the hallways to view exceptional works of art by private tour. Diane Miller, who passed away in 2013, was an ardent fan of early Belle Époque advertising art, California landscape painters such as Thomas Hill, and other artists. A portion of her collection is on display—a tribute to her life and legacy in Napa Valley wine country.

St. Supéry Estate Vineyards & Winery

Well before guests enjoy their first sip of wine, the combination of balance and elegance that informs St. Supéry's every endeavor is already in evidence. Neatly trimmed camphor trees, themselves flanked by smartly coiffed Merlot and Cabernet Sauvignon vines, line the driveway off St. Helena Highway that pierces east toward the site's oldest structure, an 1882 Queen Anne Victorian sometimes used for private tastings. Farther along lies a well-tended culinary garden that fronts the contemporary ivy-covered winery and tasting space. Depending on the season, the garden's figs, plums, tomatoes, onions, and other edibles might be ready for use in St. Supéry's food-and-wine pairings. Just past the garden, a park, complete with café tables, foun- tains, potted plants, and courts for playing *pétanque*, strikes a perky Parisian pose befitting the winery's Gallic origins and future.

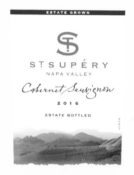

St. Supéry was founded in 1982, when Robert Skalli, scion of a famous French wine company, purchased the 1,500-acre Dollarhide Ranch, a former cattle and horse farm in the northeast- ern hills of Napa Valley. Now planted with 500 acres of mostly Bordeaux varietals — Sauvignon Blanc and Sémillon on the white side, and Cabernet Sauvignon, Malbec, Petit Verdot, and Cabernet Franc on the red. Outside the Bordeaux realm, St. Supéry makes Chardonnays (oaked and unoaked), from Dollarhide grapes, along with a light and lively Moscato. Skalli later bought the Rutherford property, thirty-eight of whose fifty-six acres are devoted to red-wine grapes. With its classic "Rutherford dust" soil adding vague hints of chocolate, this valley-floor fruit complements the ranch's tannic, earthier notes in reds containing grapes from both estates. St. Supéry also makes wines with grapes solely from Rutherford or Dollarhide.

In 2015 Skalli sold St. Supéry to the French luxury brand Chanel, which has continued the Bordeaux emphasis and the commitment to green vineyard and winery practices. Although it is highly satisfying to drop by simply to taste, reserving space at one of several interactive educational experiences is worth considering. A longtime favorite is Aromatherapy with a Corkscrew, a diverting exercise in identifying wines' aromas and how the sense of smell affects our experience of wine. Veggies + Vino, a seated tasting, presents small vegetarian bites made from seasonal produce — harvested from Dollarhide Estate Ranch and the winery's Culinary Garden — alongside estate wines and demonstrates the many creative possibilities for vegetable and wine pairings. These and a few other sessions are thoughtfully conceived and presented with style by the winery's unfailingly gracious hosts.

St. Supéry Estate Vineyards & Winery
8440 St. Helena Hwy.
(Hwy. 29)
Rutherford, CA 94573
707-963-4507
reservations@stsupery.com
stsupery.com

Owner: Chanel, Inc.

Location: .5 mile south of Rutherford Cross Rd.

Appellations: Rutherford and Napa Valley.

Hours: 10 a.m.–5 p.m. daily.

Tastings: $35 for Winemaker's Selection Tasting of 4 wines, reservations preferred; other tastings from $55 for 4 or 5 wines, reservations required.

Tours: Some educational experiences include house, garden, or other tours.

The Wines: Cabernet Franc, Cabernet Sauvignon, Chardonnay, Malbec, Merlot, Moscato, Petit Verdot, Sauvignon Blanc, Sémillon.

Specialties: Estate-grown Bordeaux-style single-vineyard wines; Virtù (white blend of Sémillon and Sauvignon Blanc); Élu (red Bordeaux blend).

Winemakers: Michael Scholz, vice president of winemaking; Brooke Shenk, winemaker.

Annual Production: Unavailable.

Of Special Note: Art gallery with changing exhibitions. Winery has dog-friendly options. All wines from grapes grown on the Rutherford or Dollarhide estate vineyards. Some wines available only in tasting room. Vineyards and winery awarded Napa Green certification.

Nearby Attraction: Culinary Institute of America at Greystone (cooking demonstrations).

STAG'S LEAP WINE CELLARS

STAG'S LEAP WINE CELLARS
5766 Silverado Trail
Napa, CA 94558
707-261-6410
tours@cask23.com
cask23.com

OWNER: Ste. Michelle Wine Estates.

LOCATION: 8 miles north of downtown Napa, 2.25 miles south of Yountville Cross Rd.

APPELLATION: Stags Leap District.

HOURS: 10 A.M.–4:30 P.M. daily.

TASTINGS: $45 for Estate Collection Tasting Flight of 4 wines; $95 for Fire & Water Tour and Tasting of 4 wines, plus cave tour and small bites (weekdays year-round and some weekends June–Oct., by appointment); $175 for Cellarius Kitchen Experience, tasting of 4 wines, plus cave tour and gourmet plates (seasonal on some weekdays, by appointment).

TOURS: Estate Wine Tasting & Cave Tour ($75), daily at 11 A.M., by appointment.

THE WINES: Cabernet Sauvignon, Chardonnay, Merlot, Sauvignon Blanc.

SPECIALTY: Estate-grown Cabernet Sauvignon.

WINEMAKER: Marcus Notaro.

ANNUAL PRODUCTION: Unavailable.

OF SPECIAL NOTE: Educational and historical exhibits about S.L.V. and FAY vineyards and the 1976 Judgment of Paris blind tasting. Visitor center and caves designed by renowned Spanish architect Javier Barba.

NEARBY ATTRACTION: Napa Valley Museum (winemaking displays, art exhibits).

The Stag's Leap Wine Cellars story is the stuff of legend, starting with the winery's name. In a two-century-old Wappo Indian myth, a magnificent stag escaped pursuing hunters by leaping through a notch in the palisades above the present-day vineyards. More recent and verifiable lore involves the 1976 Judgment of Paris blind tasting of French and California wines. Renowned Gallic critics, confident they were endorsing a homegrown wine, bestowed top honors on the 1973 Stag's Leap Wine Cellars Cabernet Sauvignon. This victory, along with that of Calistoga's Chateau Montelena for the Chardonnay presented at the same event, catapulted the Napa Valley into international prominence.

Guests at the stone and glass FAY Outlook & Visitor Center, designed by the acclaimed Spanish architect Javier Barba, can view both the Stags Leap Palisades and a sliver of the famous vineyard, now dubbed S.L.V. (for Stag's Leap Vineyard), where most of the prize-winning wine's grapes were grown. A small percentage came from the vineyard in full view, which Stag's Leap Wine Cellars founder, Warren Winiarski, christened FAY to honor the Fay family. The vintner purchased the land from these local farmers in the mid-1980s. He bought S.L.V. in 1970 in part because the FAY grapes tasted so good. Barba incorporated large stones excavated from both vineyards into the visitor center's walls.

Through a geological quirk, the FAY and S.L.V. vineyards, though side by side, have vastly dissimilar soils. S.L.V.'s are volcanic from the upheavals that created the palisades; FAY's are alluvial from a creek that flows down from them. The soils and their effect on grapes are the focus of the Fire & Water Tour and Tasting, which provides an overview of the Stag's Leap Wine Cellars' history and deep connection to its storied vineyards. Fire & Water begins with a tour of the winery's cave, followed by a private seated tasting starring the current S.L.V. and FAY Cabernets and CASK 23, a best-of-the-best blend of grapes from the two vineyards. The accompanying small bites illustrate how food friendly Stag's Leap Wine Cellars wines are. The cave is also a stop on the seasonal Cellarius Kitchen Experience, which features the same wines with larger gourmet plates prepared by the winery's executive chef.

Reservations are required for tastings that involve food or cave tours, but walk-ins are welcome for the Estate Collection Tasting Flight, offered in the main visitor space or on one of the shaded patios, prime spots to enjoy vineyard and palisades views and reflect on this pivotal winery's role in Napa Valley history.

STAGS' LEAP WINERY

To visit the Manor House at Stags' Leap Winery is to enter a world of Old California–style wealth, set amid 240 acres of pristine countryside. Like an elegant time capsule, the Romanesque mansion evokes the lavish dinners and lawn parties staged by its builder, San Francisco investor Horace B. Chase. Constructed in 1892 of locally quarried stone, the two-story house stands at the end of a driveway lined with fan palms and the low rock walls of terraced gardens. Mortared stone columns support the roof of a wraparound porch, and a castellated half-turret hosts a massive wisteria vine.

The Chases dubbed the estate Stag's Leap, a name attributed to a native Wappo legend of a stag leaping to elude hunters. The mountains behind the property then came to be called the Stags Leap Palisades. Producing wine to sell and share with friends, the Chases introduced the Stags' Leap Winery label in 1893. The Grange family bought the property in 1913 and turned it into a busy resort. The house sat empty from the early 1950s to 1970, when Carl Doumani spent four years restoring it. He revived the Stags' Leap Winery label, and in 1989 the Stags Leap District appellation (sans apostrophe) was recognized. Visitors are greeted by friendly and informative staff who take

them on a tour of the historic Manor House and the grounds. Paths winding among perennial gardens and vegetable beds offer views of the eighty-acre estate vineyard opposite the house. Inside the gracious Manor House, guests enjoy a seated tasting in the formal dining room, where soft light filters through Victorian lead glass windows. Tastings are also held outdoors on a covered patio.

Bordeaux-born Christophe Paubert joined Stags' Leap Winery as winemaker in 2009, bringing an impressive background that includes serving as cellar master at the renowned Château d'Yquem in his native France and building a winery and overhauling a large vineyard in Chile. At Stags' Leap, he crafts balanced wines with the district's characteristic depth and soft tannins. His signature is the award-winning "The Leap" Cabernet Sauvignon, made from fruit sourced from a small, distinct vineyard block at the heart of the estate, whose well-drained volcanic soil is one factor that contributes to the reputation of the winery's Cabernet Sauvignon.

Reaching an elevation of 2,000 feet, the Stags Leap Palisades form a small, secluded valley. To find the winery, visitors take an unmarked Silverado Trail turnoff and travel a narrow country road between vineyards and walnut orchards. The effort is worth it—for Stags' Leap Winery glimmers with the magic of that mighty buck.

STAGS' LEAP WINERY
6150 Silverado Trail
Napa, CA 94558
707-257-5790
stagsleap.com

OWNER: Treasury Wine Estates.

LOCATION: 7 miles north of downtown Napa.

APPELLATION: Stags Leap District.

HOURS: By appointment.

TASTINGS: $65 for 5 wines, as part of tour, by appointment.

TOURS: 90-minute Estate Tour and Tasting. Reservations required.

THE WINES: Cabernet Sauvignon, Chardonnay, Merlot, Petite Sirah, Rosé, Viognier.

SPECIALTIES: Cabernet Sauvignon, Ne Cede Malis (old-vine Petite Sirah blend).

WINEMAKER: Christophe Paubert.

ANNUAL PRODUCTION: 100,000 cases.

OF SPECIAL NOTE: One of Napa Valley's oldest wineries. Historic Manor House built in 1892.

NEARBY ATTRACTION: Napa Valley Museum (winemaking displays, art exhibits).

STERLING VINEYARDS

STERLING VINEYARDS
1111 Dunaweal Ln.
Calistoga, CA 94515
800-726-6136
sterlingvineyards.com

OWNER: Treasury Wine Estates.

LOCATION: 1 mile southeast of Calistoga.

APPELLATION: Calistoga.

HOURS: 10 A.M.–5 P.M. daily.

TASTINGS: $35 admission for aerial tram ride, self-guided tour, 5 wine tastes, and souvenir Riedel glass. For additional tastings of reserve and limited-release wines, visit the website.

TOURS: Self-guided.

THE WINES: Cabernet Sauvignon, Chardonnay, Merlot, Pinot Noir, Sauvignon Blanc, sparkling wine, Zinfandel.

SPECIALTIES: Malvasia Bianca, Cabernet Sauvignon, Platinum (Bordeaux blend).

WINEMAKER: Harry Hansen.

ANNUAL PRODUCTION: Unavailable.

OF SPECIAL NOTE: Display of Ansel Adams photographs and wine-related art.

NEARBY ATTRACTIONS: Robert Louis Stevenson Museum (author memorabilia); Napa Valley Museum (winemaking displays, art exhibits).

An eye-catching complex of bright white walls and curved bell towers, Sterling Vineyards crowns a forested volcanic knoll three hundred feet above the Napa Valley floor. The winery, which from a distance could double as a hilltop Greek island monastery, commands sweeping views of the geometric vineyards and foothills below. To reach it, visitors leave their cars in the parking lot and board an aerial gondola—the only one of its kind in the valley—for a solar-powered glide over a glistening pond, pines, and live oaks to a walkway among the treetops.

A self-guided tour encourages visitors to explore the stately facility at their own pace, while strategically stationed hosts pour wine samples along the way. Illustrated signboards describe points of interest, and motion-activated flat-screen televisions display videos of wine-making activity. Bells from a former tenth-century London church chime on the quarter hour, their rich tones ringing across exterior footpaths that afford elevated views of the crush pad and fermentation area. Inside the winery, visitors may observe employees at work among stainless-steel tanks and peek at some of the winery's 25,000 barrels as they impart delicate flavors to the wine aging within. On the South View Terrace, redwood planters brim with lavender and ornamental grasses, and two sixty-foot-tall Italian cypresses frame the scene to the south. Here, guests sip wine as they take in the panoramic vistas of vineyards, neighboring estates, and parts of the Mayacamas Mountains on the Sonoma-Napa border, where Mount St. Helena rises above the neighboring peaks to an elevation of 4,344 feet.

Englishman Peter Newton, founder of Sterling Paper International, started the winery in 1964, when he bought a fifty-acre pasture just north of the town of Calistoga. He surprised local vintners by planting Merlot—at the time considered a minor blending grape—along with Chardonnay, Cabernet Sauvignon, and Sauvignon Blanc. Five years later, Newton bottled his first wines, which included California's earliest vintage-dated Merlot. In the early 1980s, the winery purchased one thousand vineyard acres on fourteen different Napa Valley ranches, giving the winemaker a broad spectrum of fruit to work with, as well as control over the farming of the grapes. The winery continues to source fruit from these and two hundred additional acres of select Napa Valley vineyards in various appellations such as Calistoga, St. Helena, Rutherford, and Carneros.

Visitors should make touring the hilltop winery their top priority, as it is one of the most memorable experiences in the Napa Valley.

STEWART CELLARS

A valley oak more than a century old towers above Stewart Cellars' trio of rough-hewn stone buildings along downtown Yountville's Washington Street. Completed in 2016, the structures — two of them tasting spaces, the third an independently operated café — evoke ancient Scottish ruins, a nod to the heritage of the family behind this winery that debuted in 1999. The sleight of hand continues with whimsical faux-biographical interiors by Ken Fulk, whose offhand sophistication complements the soulful Cabernets of winemaker Blair Guthrie.

After selling the Houston-based computer-hardware company he'd spent twenty-five years developing, winery founder Michael Stewart sought to parlay his love of wine into a second career. His favorite Cabernet was by the respected winemaker and asked him to make the first was the immediate response, ner with Stewart, apparently a since become one of Hobbs's Hobbs's impact on the

Paul Hobbs, so he contacted international consultant and Stewart wines. Absolutely not but Hobbs agreed to have dinner charmer because Stewart has longest-standing clients. Stewarts' lives extends beyond his enological expertise. When the Stewarts' daughter, Caroline, expressed interest in winemaking, Hobbs enlisted her for harvests in Argentina and Australia and at his Sonoma County vineyards. Early on, she met Guthrie, a Hobbs protégé who studied graphic arts in his native New Zealand before gravitating to winemaking. He's now her husband. These days Caroline handles winery-related matters for Stewart Cellars; her brother, James, oversees sales and distribution.

Stewart Cellars offers several tastings. The Portfolio Flight — whites, reds (Cabernet Sauvignon, Malbec, Merlot, and Pinot Noir), and, when available, a rosé — provides a solid introduction. This flight and a reds-only one are served in the Tasting Hall, a high-ceilinged space anchored by an ultramodern cast-concrete horseshoe bar. Options across the courtyard in the plush Nomad Heritage Library include an all-Cabernet tasting and the Portfolio wines paired with chocolate.

Through Hobbs, the Stewarts met Andy Beckstoffer, a top grape grower and the owner of six of the Napa Valley's oldest and most prestigious vineyards, among them Dr. Crane (1858) and To Kalon (1868). Stewart Cellars is among the few Napa wineries making a single-vineyard Cabernet from all six. The Beckstoffer wines, coveted by collectors, are served in the Nomad Heritage Library.

Asked how Hobbs has influenced his winemaking, Guthrie cites his mentor's precision and attention to detail. "I take that mentality and mix it with my artistic approach, and I think it makes for richer wines." Favorable notices from influential critics indicate they are inclined to agree.

STEWART CELLARS
6752 Washington St.
Yountville, CA 94599
707-963-9160
info@stewartcellars.com
stewartcellars.com

OWNERS: Stewart family.

LOCATION: Northern section of downtown Yountville.

APPELLATIONS: Napa Valley, Sonoma Coast, Sonoma Mountain.

HOURS: 11 A.M.–6 P.M. daily.

TASTINGS: $30 for Portfolio Flight of 4 wines; $40 for Red Wine Flight of 4 wines; $125 for Nomad Cabernet Sauvignon Tasting of 6 wines, reservation recommended.

TOURS: Private tours of the Beckstoffer Heritage Vineyards paired with the correlating wine.

THE WINES: Cabernet Sauvignon, Chardonnay, Malbec, Merlot, Pinot Noir, Sauvignon Blanc.

SPECIALTIES: Single-vineyard Cabernet Sauvignon, including wines from all six Andy Beckstoffer Heritage Vineyards; Sonoma Mountain Rosé of Pinot Gris and Pinot Noir; Tartan Red Blend (Cabernet Sauvignon based).

WINEMAKERS: Blair Guthrie; Paul Hobbs, consulting winemaker.

ANNUAL PRODUCTION: 5,000 cases.

OF SPECIAL NOTE: On-site Southside Yountville café open for breakfast and lunch. Sonoma Mountain Rosé and Tartan Red Blend available only in tasting room.

NEARBY ATTRACTION: Napa Valley Museum (winemaking displays, art exhibits).

TRINCHERO NAPA VALLEY

TRINCHERO NAPA VALLEY
3070 N. St. Helena Hwy.
(Hwy. 29)
St. Helena, CA 94574
707-963-1160
info@trincheronapavalley
.com
trincheronapavalley.com

OWNERS:
Trinchero family.

LOCATION: 2 miles
northwest of St. Helena.

APPELLATIONS: Atlas Peak,
Calistoga, Mt. Veeder, Napa
Valley, St. Helena.

HOURS: 10 A.M.–5 P.M. daily.

TASTINGS: Valley Floor
Flight and Mountain Flight,
in Main Tasting Room,
reservations recommended.
Winemakers Selection and
Time in a Bottle, with
cheese and charcuterie,
in Legacy Lounge, by
appointment. Taste of
Terroir seminar, by
appointment. Food and
Wine Pairing, with small
bites, by appointment only
on Friday and Saturday.

TOURS: Free tours subject
to staff availability. Tour
included with Winemakers
Selection, Time in a Bottle,
Taste of Terroir, and Food
and Wine Pairings.

THE WINES: Cabernet Franc,
Cabernet Sauvignon,
Chardonnay, Malbec,
Merlot, Petit Verdot, Petite
Sirah, Sauvignon Blanc,
Sémillon.

SPECIALTIES: Single-vineyard,
estate-grown Bordeaux-
style red wines; Signature
Cabernet Sauvignon; Forte
Red Wine (blend from
multiple estate vineyards).

WINEMAKER:
Mario Monticelli.

ANNUAL PRODUCTION:
10,000–12,000 cases.

OF SPECIAL NOTE: Napa
Valley views from outdoor
terrace. Barrel tastings
daily.

When the Trinchero family decided to erect a tasting room to honor its first two wine-making generations, the architect, Bobby Torres of the third generation, tapped St. Helena's Erin Martin to fashion the interiors. The lavish space dazzles the eye at every turn, with plush leather banquettes and chairs, commissioned artworks, and Martin's trademark mélange of antiques, vintage objets d'art, haute-contemporary furniture, and dramatic light fixtures.

Martin, whose styling of Trinchero Napa Valley contributed to her receiving a prestigious international design award in 2017, worked with Torres to incorporate pieces and themes that evoked the family's past, present, and future. In 1948 the first generation, Mario and Mary Trinchero, established the wine business, with their three children, Bob, Vera, and Roger,

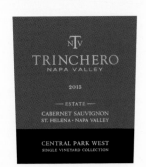

eventually playing key roles; these days the third and fourth generations are participating. Books in the public tasting room reflect Mary's love of reading, while the VIP Tasting Room's curved, backlit padded-leather bar, along with the speakeasy-like portal, acknowledges Mario's stint in an upstate New York Prohibition-era bar. The public room's way-larger-than-life antique wooden hornbill sculpture is a more symbolic recognition of Mary's and, later, Vera's contributions. To members of the Ivory Coast's Senufo tribe, says Martin, the bird reinforced a family or community's need to nurture male and female energy to survive.

The wines are as big, bold, and brimming with personality as Martin's interiors. White-wine offerings include a Sauvignon Blanc, two Chardonnays, and a Sémillon dessert wine, but reds—single-vineyard Cabernet Sauvignons meant to age; individual Cabernet Franc, Malbec, Merlot, and Petit Verdot bottlings and Petite Sirah—are the stars. Six estate vineyards, each chosen for its combination of soil, elevation, and microclimate, supply the grapes for these wines. Among four valley-floor sites is the ten-acre Cabernet Sauvignon vineyard, named for Mario Trinchero, that surrounds the tasting room. East-west across the valley from each other are two hillside vineyards at 1,500 feet, one on Atlas Peak, the other on Mount Veeder. Mario Monticelli—whose mentors include his father, a winemaker for more than four decades, and the elite Bordeaux-born consultant Philippe Melka—has made the Trinchero Napa Valley's wines since their 2007 debut.

The Taste of Terroir and Time in a Bottle tastings explore the differences between valley-floor and mountain wines. Wines paired with small bites and a Cabernet-only tasting are among the other options. Walk-in guests can choose between valley-floor and mountain tastings.

WHITEHALL LANE WINERY

cher and lavender, the colors of a California sunset, soften the geometric lines of Whitehall Lane, an angular, contemporary structure that stands in contrast to the pastoral setting of the vineyard. As if to telegraph the business at hand, the building's large windows have been cut in the shape of wine goblets. In front of the winery, a single row of square pillars runs alongside a walkway, each pillar supporting a vine that has entwined itself in the overhanging pergola.

Glass doors open into a tasting room with a white beamed ceiling, cream walls with black-and-white photos of the vineyard, black counters, and concrete bar tops. The handsome interior befits an estate where the first grapevines were planted in 1880. Even then, Napa Valley settlers were drawn to Rutherford's deep, loamy soils and sunny climate. A vestige of those days, a barn built for equipment storage, is still in use today.

In 1979 two brothers bought the twenty-six-acre vineyard and founded the winery they named after the road that runs along the south border of the property. They produced Merlot and Cabernet Sauvignon before selling the property nine years later. The Leonardini family of San Francisco took over the Whitehall Lane Estate in 1993. Tom Leonardini, already a wine aficionado, had been looking for property to purchase. He was aware of the winery's

premium vineyard sources and some of its outstanding wines. Moreover, unlike his previous enterprises, the winery presented an opportunity to create a business that could involve his entire family.

Leonardini updated the winemaking and instituted a new barrel-aging program. He also replanted the estate vineyard in Merlot and Sauvignon Blanc and began acquiring additional grape sources. Whitehall Lane now owns six Napa Valley vineyards, a total of 150 acres on the valley floor: the Estate Vineyard, the Millennium MM Vineyard, the Bommarito Vineyard, the Leonardini Vineyard, the Fawn Park Vineyard, and the Oak Glen Vineyard. The various wines produced from these vineyards were rated among the top five in the world on three occasions by *Wine Spectator* magazine.

Whitehall Lane's new building contains a barrel room and a crush pad, as well as a second-floor VIP tasting room. The goal of the facility is not to increase overall production, but to focus on small lots of Cabernet Sauvignon produced from the St. Helena and Rutherford vineyards. As the winery approaches its fortieth anniversary, the Leonardinis have many reasons to celebrate the success of their family business.

WHITEHALL LANE WINERY
1563 St. Helena Hwy. S.
St. Helena, CA 94574
707-963-9454
greatwine@
whitehalllane.com
whitehalllane.com

OWNERS:
Leonardini family.

LOCATION: 2 miles south of St. Helena.

APPELLATION: Rutherford.

HOURS: 10 A.M.–5:30 P.M. daily.

TASTINGS: $25 for current releases; price varies for reserve selections. No reservations required. Seated tastings by appointment.

TOURS: By appointment.

THE WINES: Cabernet Sauvignon, Chardonnay, dessert wine, Merlot, Pinot Noir, Sauvignon Blanc.

SPECIALTIES: Estate Cabernet Sauvignon, Leonardini Vineyard Cabernet Sauvignon, Millennium Vineyard Cabernet Sauvignon, I de V red wine.

WINEMAKER: Jason Moulton.

ANNUAL PRODUCTION: 45,000 cases.

OF SPECIAL NOTE: Limited-production Leonardini Family Selection wines available only at the winery.

NEARBY ATTRACTIONS: Bothe-Napa State Park (hiking, picnicking, horseback riding, swimming); Culinary Institute of America at Greystone (cooking demonstrations); Robert Louis Stevenson Museum (author memorabilia); Napa Valley Museum (winemaking displays, art exhibits).

YAO FAMILY WINES

YAO FAMILY WINES
929 Main St.
St. Helena, CA 94574
707-968-5874
concierge@yaofamilywines
.com
yaofamilywines.com

OWNER: Yao Ming.

LOCATION: Downtown St. Helena, west side of Main St., next to Gott's Roadside.

APPELLATION: Napa Valley.

HOURS: 10 A.M.–5 P.M. daily.

TASTINGS: Access, $35 for 3 wines; Reserve, $50 for 3 red wines; Library, $80 for vertical tasting of 3 red wines from different vintages. Reserve and library wines paired with artisan cheese and charcuterie plate.

TOURS: None.

THE WINES: Cabernet Sauvignon, Sauvignon Blanc.

SPECIALTY: Yao Ming Family Reserve Cabernet Sauvignon.

WINEMAKER: Tom Hinde.

ANNUAL PRODUCTION: 4,000 cases.

OF SPECIAL NOTE: Collection of Yao Ming NBA and Olympics basketball memorabilia on display. Glass-art chandelier by Rey Viquez, Los Angeles architect. Napa Crest Sauvignon Blanc and pre-2012 library Cabernet Sauvignon available only at tasting room.

NEARBY ATTRACTIONS: Culinary Institute of America at Greystone (cooking demonstrations); Bale Grist Mill State Historic Park (water-powered mill circa 1846); Robert Louis Stevenson Museum (author memorabilia).

A few months before his 2016 induction into basketball's hall of fame, the former NBA star Yao Ming waxed poetic about the "music on the court" that mesmerized him as an adolescent in China. He recalled with joy "the songs players hear" when their shoes scrape the floor, the ball swooshes through the net, competitors' muscles make contact, and how "you can hear your heart beat." As the starting center of the Houston Rockets, the seven-foot-six Yao spent many postgame evenings at Texas-style steak houses, along the way developing a similar passion for collector-quality Napa Valley Cabernet Sauvignon—so much so the Shanghai-born superstar established a winery whose debut 2009 vintage was released in 2011, the year he retired as a pro player.

Wineries owned by celebrities can be problematic affairs, but Yao assembled a top-notch team led by Tom Hinde, a respected winemaker whose experience ranges from smaller operations such as Flowers, a Chardonnay and Pinot Noir producer along the Sonoma Coast, to the megabrand Kendall-Jackson. For Yao Family Wines, Hinde focuses on Cabernet Sauvignon and other Bordeaux varietals under two labels, Yao Ming and Napa Crest.

The flagship wines are two Yao Ming Cabernet Sauvignons, one a reserve wine with grapes sourced from several Napa Valley subappellations. Aged the past few vintages in 100 percent new French oak for twenty-four months, the reserve consistently earns high scores from wine critics. The other Cab has been well received, too. You can imagine these wines with a steak or aged Gouda, but they're highly drinkable on their own. The accessible Napa Crest line includes a Sauvignon Blanc and a Cabernet-dominant proprietary red blend, both reasonably priced given the level of quality.

All tasting flights at Yao Family Wines, whose tasting room on downtown St. Helena's southern edge opened in 2016, include at least one of the flagship Cabernets. As with the other wines, these can be purchased by the glass as well. Though built for a previous tenant, the expansive space, with its large skylight, subdued shades of gray, up-lit quartz tasting bar, and art-installation chandelier made of two hundred China-red wine bottles, seems designed expressly for Yao.

The space provides a perfect showcase for the sports star's multifaceted interests. As prominent as the basketball memorabilia are photographs of the ex-player engaged in humanitarian projects that include educational outreach and the rescue and support of endangered rhinoceroses, elephants, and sharks. After tasting his wines and learning about his sports career and altruism, one gets the impression that the drive to excel with class and sensitivity is the unifying element.

SONOMA

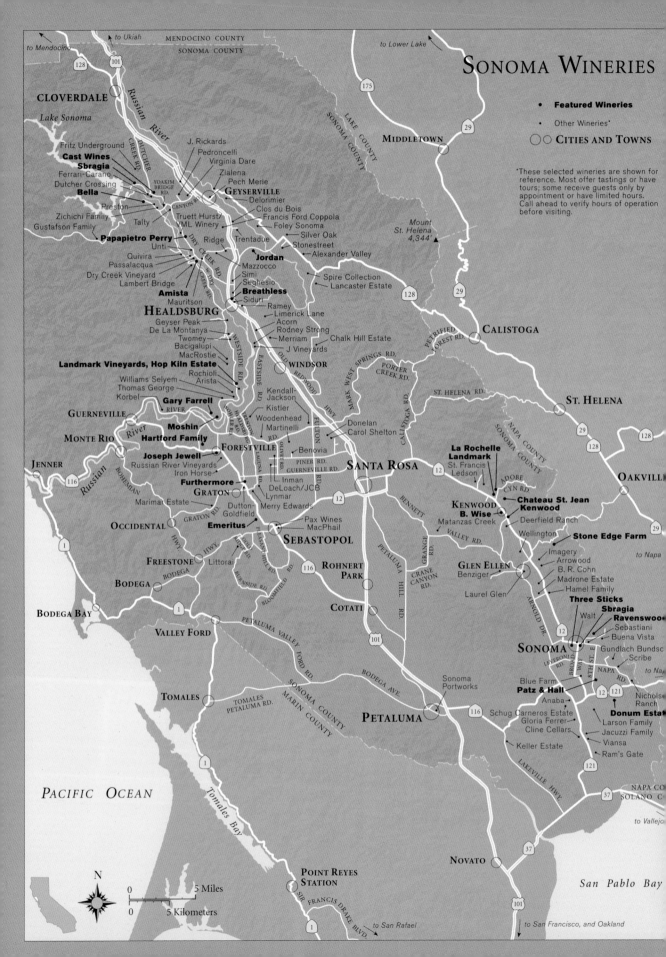

SONOMA WINERIES

- **●** **Featured Wineries**
- **·** Other Wineries*
- ◯◯ **CITIES AND TOWNS**

*These selected wineries are shown for reference. Most offer tastings or have tours; some receive guests only by appointment or have limited hours. Call ahead to verify hours of operation before visiting.

to Mendocino
to Ukiah
MENDOCINO COUNTY
SONOMA COUNTY
to Lower Lake

CLOVERDALE
Lake Sonoma
Russian River

Fritz Underground
Cast Wines
Sbragia
Ferrari-Carano
Dutcher Crossing
Bella
Preston
Zichichi Family
Gustafson Family
Talty
Papapietro Perry
Unti
Quivira
Passalacqua
Dry Creek Vineyard
Lambert Bridge
Amista
Mauritson

DUTCHER CREEK RD.
YOAKIM BRIDGE RD.
CANYON RD.
DRY CREEK RD.
WEST DRY CREEK RD.

J. Rickards
Pedroncelli
Virginia Dare
Zialena
Pech Merle
GEYSERVILLE
Delorimier
Clos du Bois
Francis Ford Coppola
Foley Sonoma
Trentadue
Silver Oak
Stonestreet
Alexander Valley
Ridge
Jordan
Mazzocco
Simi
Seghesio
Breathless
Siduri

Mount St. Helena 4,344'

MIDDLETOWN

LAKE COUNTY
SONOMA COUNTY

Spire Collection
Lancaster Estate

CALISTOGA

PETRIFIED FOREST RD.

HEALDSBURG
Geyser Peak
De La Montanya
Twomey
Bacigalupi
MacRostie
Landmark Vineyards, Hop Kiln Estate
Rochioli
Williams Selyem
Thomas George
Arista
Korbel
Gary Farrell

WESTSIDE RD.
EASTSIDE RD.
OLD REDWOOD HWY.

Ramey
Limerick Lane
Acorn
Rodney Strong
Merriam
J Vineyards
Chalk Hill Estate

MARK WEST SPRINGS RD.
PORTER CREEK RD.
ST. HELENA RD.

ST. HELENA

GUERNEVILLE
River
Russian River
Moshin
Hartford Family

Kendall Jackson
Kistler
Woodenhead
Martinelli

WINDSOR
FULTON RD.

Donelan
Carol Shelton

NAPA COUNTY
SONOMA COUNTY

OAKVILLE

MONTE RIO

JENNER
Russian River
Bohemian Hwy.

Joseph Jewell
Russian River Vineyards
Iron Horse
Furthermore
GRATON
Marimar Estate

FORESTVILLE
LAGUNA RD.
PINER RD.
GUERNEVILLE RD.
Benovia
Inman
DeLoach/JCB
Lynmar
Merry Edwards

SANTA ROSA

La Rochelle
Landmark
St. Francis
Ledson

ADOBE CANYON RD.

Chateau St. Jean
Kenwood
B. Wise
Matanzas Creek
Deerfield Ranch
Wellington

Stone Edge Farm

29

to Napa

OCCIDENTAL
GRATON RD.
Emeritus

Dutton Goldfield
Pax Wines
MacPhail

SEBASTOPOL

KENWOOD
GLEN ELLEN
Benziger
Laurel Glen

Imagery
Arrowood
B. R. Cohn
Madrone Estate
Hamel Family

to Napa

FREESTONE
BODEGA HWY.
Littoral

ROHNERT PARK

Three Sticks
Sbragia
Walt
Ravenswood
Sebastiani
Buena Vista
Gundlach Bundschu
Scribe

BODEGA

COTATI

SONOMA
NAPA RD.

to Napa

BODEGA BAY

VALLEY FORD

PETALUMA VALLEY FORD RD.
BURNSIDE RD.
BLOOMFIELD RD.

PETALUMA HILL RD.
CRANE CANYON RD.
GRANGE RD.

Blue Farm
Patz & Hall
Anaba
Schug Carneros Estate
Gloria Ferrer
Cline Cellars
Keller Estate

Nicholson Ranch
Donum Estate
Larson Family
Jacuzzi Family
Viansa
Ram's Gate

TOMALES
TOMALES PETALUMA RD.
SONOMA COUNTY
MARIN COUNTY

BODEGA AVE.

Sonoma Portworks

PETALUMA

LAKEVILLE HWY.

NAPA CO
SOLANO CO

to Vallejo

PACIFIC OCEAN

Tomales Bay

NOVATO

San Pablo Bay

N
0   5 Miles
0   5 Kilometers

POINT REYES STATION

SIR FRANCIS DRAKE BLVD.

to San Rafael

to San Francisco, and Oakland

S onoma boasts the greatest geographical diversity in California wine country. From the Pacific Coast to the inland valleys, to the Mayacamas Mountains that define the eastern border with Napa County, the countryside is crisscrossed by dozens of rural roads, making it an ideal destination for casual exploration.

Most of the county's oldest wineries can be found in the historic town of Sonoma. Facing the extensively landscaped eight-acre central plaza are nineteenth-century adobe and false-front buildings that now  house upscale shops, restaurants, and inns, as well as historic sites.

In the northern part of the county, the city of Healdsburg has evolved from a quiet backwater into the hottest destina- tion in Sonoma County. It sits at the hub of three major grape-growing regions — Russian River Valley, Alexander Valley, and Dry Creek Valley — all within a ten-minute drive of the vibrant town plaza.

North of Santa Rosa, the Russian River Valley extends from the Healdsburg area almost all the way to the ocean, where West Sonoma Coast has become a highly regarded appellation. In addition to the colorful villages clustered along the coastal routes, the region offers boat- ing, swimming, and fishing opportunities and the shade of giant redwoods that soar above the Russian River's banks.

WELCOME
11-4:30

Cheers!

AMISTA VINEYARDS

When Mike and Vicky Farrow met in 1982, they had a common dream: to own a vineyard and make wines to share with friends. In 1994 they planted their first vineyard at their Bay Area home. Mike, a chemist with a passion for cooking and wine, also purchased a half ton of Cabernet Sauvignon grapes and produced wine in the driveway. Both Mike and Vicky enjoyed the experience and talked about expanding the venture. However, Vicky accepted a job offer in New Jersey, and the couple had to say goodbye to the nascent vineyard. Over the years, Mike continued to hone his winemaking skills through self-education and visits to vineyards in Northern California and Europe. He also scoured real estate ads for vineyard properties. He eventually found an ideal site with twenty acres of Chardon- nay vines in Sonoma County's Dry Creek Valley, which the couple purchased in 1999.

The Farrows immediately embarked on vineyard im- provement plans and dove into the winemaking business. They replanted eight acres with Syrah and finally were able to move to the property in 2002. In 2003 Mike harvested estate Syrah and purchased Zinfandel and Cabernet Sauvignon grapes from Healdsburg neighbors, then used a nearby custom-crush and winemaking service to produce single-vineyard wines. Amista Vineyards was established in 2005, the same year its 2003 wines, from the above fruit plus estate Chardonnay, were released. They chose the name Amista, a Spanish word that roughly translates to "making friends," in part to recognize the area's original settlers. The vineyard straddles the boundaries of two former Mexican land grant ranchos, Rancho Tzabaco and Rancho Sotoyome.

Today, Amista Vineyards produces six sparkling wines—using the traditional French *méthode champenoise*—and six still wines. It is the only estate sparkling house in Dry Creek Valley. In 2011 Mike handed the head winemaker reins to Ashley Herzberg, whose bottlings are lauded for their elegant style and neutral oak influences. Much of the fruit comes from the estate, which focuses on Rhône varietals: Grenache, Syrah, and Mourvèdre. Nine acres of Chardonnay produce grapes for the winery's single-vineyard Chardonnay and sparkling wines such as the Fusión cuvée.

Visitors taste the wines at the spacious tasting barn and courtyard, opened in 2007. The interior has colorful works by local artists. An upbeat vibe prevails indoors, where popcorn pops all day every weekend, and outdoors, where the patio offers vineyard views. Amista Vineyards has created habitat to foster the regeneration of endangered steelhead trout and coho salmon in Dry Creek, which runs through the property. Visitors can join a vineyard tour or follow a self-guided walk through the historic land that provided a dream come true for Mike and Vicky Farrow.

AMISTA VINEYARDS
3320 Dry Creek Rd.
Healdsburg, CA 95448
707-431-9200
tr@amistavineyards.com
amistavineyards.com

OWNERS: Mike and Vicky Farrow.

LOCATION: About 5 miles northwest of downtown Healdsburg.

APPELLATIONS: Dry Creek Valley, Rockpile.

HOURS: 11 A.M.–4:30 P.M. daily.

TASTINGS: $15 for 4 wines; $30 for flight of 3 sparkling wines and 1 estate selection.

TOURS: Self-guided Vineyard Adventure Walk. Guided tour and tasting, $45, daily at 11 A.M.

THE WINES: Blanc de Blanc, vintage Blanc de Blanc, Fusión cuvée, Grenache, Mataró (Mourvèdre), and Syrah sparkling wines. Cabernet Sauvignon, Chardonnay, Grenache, Mourvèdre, Syrah, and Zinfandel still wines.

SPECIALTIES: Sparkling wines (*méthode champenoise*), Tres (GSM blend: Grenache, Syrah, Mourvèdre).

WINEMAKER: Ashley Herzberg.

ANNUAL PRODUCTION: About 2,800 cases.

OF SPECIAL NOTE: Tent-shaded and open picnic areas; pétanque court. Small gift selection. Wine-and-food pairing, $50 per person, by appointment. Wine and cheese platter for two, $50. Zinfandel and Chocolate pairing, $35 per person. Only US winery making sparkling Mourvèdre. Winery is pet friendly. All wines available only in tasting room.

NEARBY ATTRACTIONS: Lake Sonoma; Russian River.

B. WISE VINEYARDS

B. WISE VINEYARDS
9077 Sonoma Hwy.
(Hwy. 12)
Kenwood, CA 95452
707-282-9169
bwisevineyards.com

OWNERS: Brion and
Ronda Wise.

LOCATION: 11 miles northwest of Sonoma, 12 miles
east of Santa Rosa.

APPELLATIONS: Moon
Mountain District Sonoma
County, Sonoma Valley,
Fort Ross–Seaview.

HOURS: 10:30 A.M.–4:30 P.M.
daily.

TASTINGS: Kenwood Tasting
Flight, $20 for 3 or 4 wines.
Reserve Flight, $65 for 3 or
4 wines.

TOURS: Winery and cave
tour by appointment only;
call or ask at tasting room.

THE WINES: Cabernet
Franc, Cabernet Sauvignon,
Chardonnay, Petite Sirah,
Pinot Noir, Syrah, Tannat,
Zinfandel.

SPECIALTIES: Cabernet
Sauvignon, Pinot Noir,
single-vineyard Cabernet
Sauvignon, Trios (Cabernet
blend), Wisdom Red Blend.

WINEMAKERS: Massimo
Monticelli and
Mark Herold.

ANNUAL PRODUCTION:
5,000 cases.

OF SPECIAL NOTE: Moon
Mountain District cave tour
and tasting by appointment.
Most wines available only at
tasting room.

NEARBY ATTRACTIONS:
Annadel State Park (hiking,
biking); Quarryhill
Botanical Garden (Asian
plant collection); Sugarloaf
Ridge State Park (hiking,
camping, horseback riding).

A red sculpture fashioned of wine-barrel hoops marks the tasting space of B. Wise Vineyards, an accomplished producer of artisanal red wines. The decor—cowhide sofa and matching chairs, ceramic tile floor, and poured-concrete bar supported by rough-hewn eucalyptus beams—creates a comfortably chic setting for sipping the Cabernet Sauvignon, Pinot Noir, and other wines of fourth-generation winemaker Massimo Monticelli. Mark Herold, who made his reputation crafting the Napa Valley's Merus Cabernet and other cult wines, collaborates on the Cabernets with Monticelli, himself a veteran of the acclaimed Silver Oak Cellars.

The winery's lowercase "b. wise" logo seems a whimsical admonition to behave intelligently, but it's also a play on vintner Brion Wise's name. Wise grew up on an apple farm in Yakima, Washington, long before that area was known for wine, though the family grew grapes for homemade bottlings. He became a chemical engineer, but memories of winemaking intensified into a yearning to own a vineyard. In 2002 Wise bought a hundred-acre parcel on the western slope of the Mayacamas Mountains.

Wise's land, within the Sonoma Valley's Moon Mountain District, sits adjacent to the historic Monte Rosso Vineyard, established in 1880. *Monte rosso* means "red mountain," in this case in recognition of the area's thin layer of red volcanic ash soil that delivers bold, mineral-driven flavors. Wine collectors covet the Brion Monte Rosso Cabernet from grapes Wise purchases from this vineyard. He planted his own vineyard, twenty-one acres total, mainly to Cabernet Sauvignon, Zinfandel, and Syrah, with smaller amounts of Merlot, Petit Verdot, and other varietals used in wines such as the reasonably priced Wisdom Red Blend of all five.

Given Wise's agricultural background, it should come as no surprise that farming is a passion. His extensive preparatory research included determining, for instance, which Cabernet Sauvignon clones would perform best in particular vineyard sections. The flavors of different clones, or variants, of the varietal provide Monticelli and Herold a broad palette when assembling their wines, which also benefit from recent innovations in crop management and fermentation and aging techniques.

Guests at the airy Kenwood space, designed by Brion's wife, Ronda, sample flights of three or four wines. Monticelli also makes a sophisticated Chardonnay from grapes grown in the coastal Fort Ross–Seaview appellation. He shows himself equally adept working with Pinot Noir, achieving a lush mouthfeel yet retaining the varietal's delicacy and floral aromatics. As with the other B. Wise offerings, for all the agricultural and technical know-how, the lasting impression is of sheer artistry.

BELLA VINEYARDS AND WINE CAVES

Located on the banks of Dry Creek, this rustic winery has a fairy-tale quality. The refurbished, red-sided barn; the ancient olive trees with their giant, gnarled trunks; and the historic vineyard thriving above the cave entrance could be an illustration right out of an old-fashioned children's book.

The tale is a romantic one with a happily-ever-after ending. In 1994 Lynn and Scott Adams came to the Sonoma wine country to get married and fell in love all over again—with the land. They made another vow: to live in a rural setting and produce fine red wine. After all, Dry Creek Valley has long been famous for its yielding lush and complex wines. A their first Zinfandel vineyard, on end. Before long, the Adamses property and spent several years Davis. By the time they opened to call the place. Bella is named in who arrived around the same

Bella
LILY HILL ESTATE
dry creek valley zinfandel

very old Zinfandel vines known for year later, the young couple bought 115 acres at the valley's western moved to the area to manage the taking viticulture classes at UC the winery, they knew exactly what honor of their first two daughters, time as their first wine barrels.

The Adamses' dream of hand-Zinfandel has remained their focus. the old-vine Zinfandel vineyard in

crafting small lots of exceptional At the heart of it is Lily Hill Estate, Dry Creek Valley and home to their

winery. In 1915 Italian immigrant Adamo Micheli and his young son, Angelo, planted the first vines on Lily Hill with a horse and plow. Angelo and the young vines grew up together, and he continued to watch over the land with his own children for the next several decades. Believing that every great vineyard has its own story to tell, the Adamses craft their wines with a minimal approach that allows the land to shine through. Bella does not need huge crops to make its wines—in fact, quite the opposite. The first vintage, 1999, consisted of only two hundred cases. The Adamses have continued to make single-vineyard wines in small lots to showcase the special qualities of each vineyard they work with. The winery remains focused on its own century-old vineyard, along with prized sites tended by other dedicated winegrowers.

Tastings at this low-key and welcoming winery are conducted inside the high-ceilinged aging caves, which are decorated with antique winery artifacts from around the world. One of the winery's tours takes guests, via four-wheel-drive vehicles, to the top of the Lily Hill Estate vineyard for a breathtaking view of Dry Creek Valley to experience the same serenity and inspiration that Lynn and Scott Adams find in the vistas of vineyards and rolling hills.

BELLA VINEYARDS AND WINE CAVES
9711 West Dry Creek Rd.
Healdsburg, CA 95448
866-471-9880
707-395-6136
info@bellawinery.com
bellawinery.com

OWNERS: Scott and Lynn Adams.

LOCATION: 9 miles northwest of Healdsburg via Dry Creek Rd. and Yoakim Bridge Rd.

APPELLATION: Dry Creek Valley.

HOURS: 11 A.M.–4:30 P.M. daily.

TASTINGS: $20.

TOURS: Cave tour, blending tour, and 4-wheel-vehicle vineyard tour, by appointment.

THE WINES: Grenache, Petite Sirah, Syrah, Zinfandel.

SPECIALTY: Small-production, old-vine Zinfandel.

WINEMAKER: Joe Healy.

ANNUAL PRODUCTION: 7,500 cases.

OF SPECIAL NOTE: Tasting room in a 7,000-square-foot cave. Picnic area partially shaded by 100-year-old olive trees. Vineyard tours and tastings on restored vintage Land Rover Defender and Pinzgauer vehicles by appointment. Limits on the purchase of specialty production wines.

NEARBY ATTRACTION: Lake Sonoma (hiking, fishing, boating, camping, swimming).

BREATHLESS SPARKLING WINES

BREATHLESS SPARKLING WINES
499 Moore Ln.
Healdsburg, CA 95448
707-395-7300
info@breathlesswines.com
breathlesswines.com

OWNERS: Sharon Cohn, Rebecca Faust, Cynthia Faust.

LOCATION: 4 blocks west of Healdsburg Plaza via North St.

APPELLATIONS: Dry Creek Valley, Napa Valley, North Coast.

HOURS: 11 A.M.–6 P.M. Thursday–Tuesday. Wednesday by appointment.

TASTINGS: $16 for 3 wines plus 1 bonus wine. Reserve tasting TBA.

TOURS: Guided facility tour and tasting, $30, by appointment.

THE WINES: Blanc de Blancs Brut, Blanc de Noirs, Brut 2012, Brut Magnum, Brut Rosé, Chardonnay, Pinot Noir, Rosé.

SPECIALTY: Sparkling wines using *méthode champenoise*.

WINEMAKER: Penny Gadd-Coster.

ANNUAL PRODUCTION: 2,500 cases.

OF SPECIAL NOTE: Winery is pet friendly. Sabrage Experience (learn to pop open a bottle with an authentic Italian saber), $69. Breakfast at Breathless, last Sunday of month, April–October, $23. Cirque Celebration (annual 1920s-themed event), mid-September. All wines available only in tasting room. Small selection of gifts for purchase. Polaroid photo booth with props. Many special events open to public generate funds for nonprofit groups.

NEARBY ATTRACTIONS: Lake Sonoma; Russian River.

Bubbles, bling, and bliss all go hand in hand at Breathless Sparkling Wines. Three sisters—Sharon Cohn, Rebecca Faust, and Cynthia Faust—established the winery in 2011 to honor their mother, Martha, who suffered from a rare genetic flaw. Martha lacked an enzyme that prevents emphysema, and she eventually passed away from the disease, even though she had never smoked a single cigarette. "Breathless is about celebrating moments in life—big or small—that take our breath away," says Sharon Cohn, the eldest of the sister trio. Martha instilled in her daughters a passion for life and encouraged them to "dream big, live life to the fullest, and take no breath for granted," adds Sharon. Breathless Sparkling Wines embodies Martha's bubbly zest for life in the wines, in the tasting room with a bohemian flair, and in the logo, which portrays a young girl in flapper garb. "We thought she looked like she was living a breathless life," Sharon explains.

Establishing a winery was a natural progression for the three sisters, who grew up in nearby Kenwood and have longtime connections to the wine business. Sharon was involved with B.R. Cohn Winery for many years. Rebecca co-owns Rack & Riddle Custom Wine Services, an acclaimed production facility. Cynthia is manager of business development at Rack & Riddle. Winemaker and honorary sister Penny Gadd-Coster has decades of sparkling winemaking experience. In 2007 she became the winemaker for Rack & Riddle and joined Breathless Wines in 2011. She handcrafts sparkling wines from high-quality Pinot Noir and Chardonnay grapes using the traditional French method, *méthode champenoise.* Under her guidance, the winery produces fewer than 3,000 cases a year from fruit sourced from select vineyards in Sonoma, Napa, and Mendocino counties. Although sparkling wines take center stage, Breathless also makes limited quantities of Still Breathless wines: Rosé of Pinot Noir, Pinot Noir, and Chardonnay.

In 2014 Rack & Riddle moved from Hopland to a state-of-the-art facility in the new West Healdsburg Warehouse district, a short walk from the town square. The new tasting room for Breathless Sparkling Wines, made of four recycled shipping containers, opened amid a garden oasis in fall of 2016. Effervescent in every way, the venue evokes the fun and frills of the 1920s flapper era, with sparkling lights, chandeliers, mirrors, shiny tables, marble counters, and sequins. Guests can sip their wines in the cozy indoor rooms with several long high-back benches and tables or in the spacious patio. In keeping with the Breathless spirit, guests are encouraged to don 1920s-style props and snap photos with a Polaroid camera to capture the moment.

CAST WINES

North of the historic Dry Creek General Store, Dry Creek Road follows its namesake waterway's curves past more than two dozen mostly family-owned wineries. Among them is Cast Wines, a relative newcomer that opened on Memorial Day weekend in 2014. A few years earlier, its principal owners, Jack and Ann Seifrick, toured this section of the Dry Creek Valley appellation. The visit inspired Jack, at the time a Texas-based executive, to establish a winery to showcase the talents of a winemaker, Mike Gulyash, whose style captivated the couple. Within a year, Gulyash had helped Jack and Ann locate the fifteen-acre estate that became Cast Wines.

Many tastings take place in a recently constructed space whose redwood siding, burlap-covered walls, and reclaimed-wood ceiling complement the pastoral setting. On sunny days, though, guests tend to gravitate to the westward-facing terraces to take in sweeping views of Cast's six-acre Grey Palm Vineyard and, vines of Bella, Ferrari-Carano, As convivial as the setting with serious intent. This con-start at the Alexander Valley's riod when André Tchelistcheff, influential winemaker, was

across the valley, the hillside and other neighbors. is, Gulyash crafts the wines summate professional got his Jordan winery during the pe-postwar California's most consulting enologist. "Patience was the most important thing I learned from André," says Gulyash—having the faith that the right farming and cellar methods will yield superlative wines without excessive intervention. A little experience helps, too. Gulyash gained further insights while working at Sonoma Valley's B.R. Cohn Winery with Pinot Noir expert Merry Edwards during her time there as consulting winemaker.

For Cast's Pinot Noir, from the coveted Bacigalupi Vineyard, Gulyash's ability to match the right clones, or variants, of the grape with the most beneficial French oak barrels has yielded subtle wines and favorable critical notice. Gulyash proves similarly adept with Zinfandel planted next door in 1971, but Cast's Sauvignon Blanc most distinctly illustrates the winemaker's creativity.

Inspired by ice wines in British Columbia's Okanagan Valley, where he worked briefly, Gulyash ferments the Sauvignon Blanc at 45°F, a relatively low temperature, for three months or so, a process that emphasizes stone-fruit characteristics as opposed to citrusy or grassy ones. The resulting wine, novel in flavor and texture, ranks among Cast's most popular offerings. It was this "mix of artistry and science" that drew the Seifricks to Gulyash's winemaking in the first place, says Jack, along with his gift for "crafting wines that people enjoy." The couple and their tasting room crew back this up with a casual experience guests find equally satisfying.

CAST WINES
8500 Dry Creek Rd.
Geyserville, CA 95441
707-431-1225
info@castwines.com
castwines.com

OWNERS: Jack and Ann Seifrick; John and Jacki Miller.

LOCATION: 8.5 miles northwest of US 101 via Dry Creek Rd. exit.

APPELLATIONS: Dry Creek Valley, Russian River Valley.

HOURS: 10 A.M.–5 P.M. daily.

TASTINGS: $10 for 4 wines; $15 for 5 reserve wines.

TOURS: Vineyard and Cellar Tours ($50). Cast Experience Tour ($65) of vineyard (weather permitting) and cellar. All guided tours include tasting; daily by appointment.

THE WINES: Cabernet Sauvignon, Chardonnay, Petite Sirah, Pinot Noir, Sauvignon Blanc, Zinfandel.

SPECIALTIES: Old-vine Zinfandel, Rosé of Zinfandel, Invocation Petite Sirah, Zinfandel blend, Blanc de Noirs sparkling wine.

WINEMAKER: Mike Gulyash.

ANNUAL PRODUCTION: 3,500 cases.

OF SPECIAL NOTE: Outdoor terrace with vineyard views; tree-shaded picnic area near Petite Sirah vines. Cheese plates available for purchase. Cave room for seated tastings. Events include Dry Creek Passport (April), LobsterFest (June), and Paella Party (September). Winery is dog and family friendly. Most wines sold only at tasting room.

NEARBY ATTRACTION: Lake Sonoma (swimming, fishing, boating, hiking, camping).

CHATEAU ST. JEAN

CHATEAU ST. JEAN
8555 Sonoma Hwy.
(HWY. 12)
Kenwood, CA 95452
707-257-5784
chateaustjean.com

OWNER: Treasury
Wine Estates.

LOCATION: 8 miles east
of Santa Rosa.

APPELLATION:
Sonoma Valley.

HOURS: 10 A.M. – 5 P.M. daily.

TASTINGS: $15 in main
Tasting Room; $35 in
Reserve Tasting Room.

TOURS: None.

THE WINES: Cabernet
Sauvignon, Chardonnay,
Fumé Blanc, Gewürztra-
miner, Malbec, Merlot,
Pinot Blanc, Pinot Noir,
Riesling, Syrah, Viognier.

SPECIALTIES: Cinq Cépages
and vineyard-designated
wines.

WINEMAKER:
Margo Van Staaveren.

ANNUAL PRODUCTION:
500,000 cases.

OF SPECIAL NOTE: Picnic
tables in oak and redwood
grove. Store offering
gourmet food and
merchandise. Bocce ball
court.

NEARBY ATTRACTION:
Sugarloaf Ridge State
Park (hiking, camping,
horseback riding).

With the dramatic profile of Sugarloaf Ridge as a backdrop, the exquisitely landscaped grounds at Chateau St. Jean in Kenwood evoke the image of a grand country estate. The château itself dates to the 1920s, but it wasn't until 1973 that a family of Central Valley, California, growers of table grapes founded the winery. They named it after a favorite relative and, with tongue in cheek, placed a statue of "St. Jean" in the garden.

The winery building was constructed from the ground up to suit Chateau St. Jean's particular style of winemaking. The founders believed in the European practice of creating vineyard-designated wines, so they designed the winery to accommodate numerous lots of grapes, which could be kept separate throughout the winemaking process. Wines from each special vineyard are also bottled and marketed separately, with the vineyard name on the label. The winery makes a dozen vineyard-designated wines from the Sonoma Valley, Alexander Valley, Russian River Valley, and Carneros appellations. The winery also produces other premium varietals and one famously successful blend, the flagship Cinq Cépages Caber-net Sauvignon.

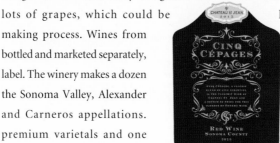

Chateau St. Jean became the first Sonoma winery to be given the prestigious Wine of the Year award from *Wine Spectator* magazine for its 1996 Cinq Cépages, a blend of the five traditional Bordeaux varietals, including Cabernet Sauvignon, Cabernet Franc, and Malbec. The winery received high acclaim again when it was given the #2 Wine of the Year award from *Wine Spectator* for its 1999 Cinq Cépages Cabernet Sauvignon. Winemaker Margo Van Staaveren has more than thirty years of vineyard and winemaking experience with Chateau St. Jean, and her knowledge of Sonoma further underscores her excellence in highlighting the best of each vineyard.

In the summer of 2000, Chateau St. Jean opened the doors to its new Visitor Center and Gardens. A formal Mediterranean-style garden contains roses, herbs, and citrus trees planted in oversize terra-cotta urns arranged to create a number of open-air "rooms." Visitors have always been welcome to relax on the winery's redwood-studded grounds, but now the setting is enhanced by the extensive garden plantings and a bocce ball court.

Beyond the Mediterranean garden is the tasting room with a custom-made tasting bar. Fashioned from mahogany with ebony accents, the thirty-five-foot-long bar is topped with sheet zinc. The elegant château houses the Reserve Tasting Room. Visitors who would like to learn more about Chateau St. Jean wines are encouraged to make a reservation for a more in-depth program.

DONUM ESTATE

Few wineries integrate winemaking, art, and agriculture as seamlessly as the Donum Estate, just north of the San Pablo Bay in the Carneros appellation. On a knoll where dairy cows once grazed, guests at private tastings sip Pinot Noirs in a simple yet elegant wood and glass hospitality building designed by Matt Hollis of the San Francisco–based MH Architects and completed in 2017. Gazing at the gently rolling, neatly coiffed vineyards, it's not difficult to understand how this landscape has captivated Anne Moller-Racke, the winery's founder and winegrower, for more than three decades.

When Moller-Racke established the Donum Estate in 2001, she had already farmed this land for more than ten years, having planted it for a previous owner. With an inaugural vintage of 150 cases, the Donum Estate quickly established a reputation for intense, refined Pinot Noirs that deftly split the difference be-

tween the overly fruity "power Pinots" popular at the time and the less assertive exem- plars of the varietal that pre- ceded them. Moller-Racke's impressive estate-only wines caught the attention of Danish investors, who purchased the winery in 2011.

The Donum Estate, which Moller-Racke still runs, produces Pinot Noir and Chardonnay from three distinctive Northern Califor- nia appellations. At nearly two hundred acres, the Carneros estate is by far the largest property. The winery also owns a smaller vineyard, Winside, in the Russian River Valley, with sixteen acres of Pinot Noir and Chardonnay, and has a long-term lease on a vineyard in Mendocino County's Anderson Valley. Seated tastings usually include a Chardonnay, followed by three or four Pinot Noirs. The hosts often open the hospitality building's tall retractable glass doors; even on the hottest days, cooling San Pablo Bay and Pacific breezes waft through. After enjoying the wines, guests stroll part of the estate, passing by Pinot Noir vines, the stone remains of an 1870s stagecoach stop, organic gardens, and some of the sculptures on display by international artists. Most tours take in the twelve large bronze depictions of the Chinese zodiac signs by Ai Weiwei, along with works by, among others, Keith Haring, Louise Bourgeois, and Anselm Kiefer.

At first, the plan was to have no more than ten artworks, but the reaction of visitors has been so positive that the collection has grown to more than forty pieces by artists from more than twenty nations. Fabricated of chrome, polished steel, and other durable materials, the artworks mirror the wines, which, like the sculptures, Moller-Racke describes as serious and made to last.

DONUM ESTATE
24500 Ramal Rd.
Sonoma, CA 95476
707-732-2200
info@thedonumestate
.com
thedonumestate.com

OWNER: Winside.

LOCATION: 7.25 miles southeast of historic Sonoma Plaza, off Carneros Hwy. 121/12.

APPELLATIONS: Los Carneros, Russian River Valley, Anderson Valley.

HOURS: Daily, by appointment.

TASTINGS: $80 for 4 or 5 wines.

TOURS: Short tour of parts of estate included with tasting.

THE WINES: Chardonnay, Pinot Noir.

SPECIALTY: Pinot Noir.

WINEMAKER: Dan Fishman.

ANNUAL PRODUCTION: 4,000 cases.

OF SPECIAL NOTE: World-class collection of sculptures placed in vineyards and elsewhere on property. Remains of an old stage-coach stop erected in 1870 on-site. Most wines avail-able only at winery.

NEARBY ATTRACTIONS: Sonoma Valley Museum of Art (modern and contem-porary art); Cornerstone Sonoma (with *Sunset* test gardens and outdoor kitchen); di Rosa (indoor and outdoor exhibits of works by contemporary Bay Area artists).

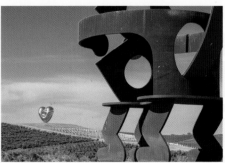

EMERITUS VINEYARDS

EMERITUS VINEYARDS
2500 Gravenstein Hwy.
North
Sebastopol, CA 95472
707-823-9463
hello@emeritusvineyards.
com
emeritusvineyards.com

OWNER: Brice Jones.

LOCATION: 3 miles north of
Sebastopol, 8 miles west
of Santa Rosa.

APPELLATIONS: Russian
River Valley, Sonoma
Coast.

HOURS: 10 A.M.–4 P.M. daily
in summer. 11 A.M.–4 P.M.
Monday–Thursday and
10:30 A.M.–4 P.M. Friday–
Sunday in winter.

TASTINGS: $25 for 4 wines.

TOURS: Vineyard and
winery tour Friday–
Monday, by appointment.

THE WINE: Pinot Noir.

SPECIALTIES: Single-
vineyard estate-grown
Pinot Noir; Rosé of
Pinot Noir.

WINEMAKER: David Lattin.

ANNUAL PRODUCTION:
8,500 cases.

OF SPECIAL NOTE: One of
Sonoma County's largest
dry-farmed vineyards.
All wines made from
dry-farmed estate grapes.
Most wines available only
at tasting room. Events
include End of Frost
(last Saturday in April)
and Harvest Trail (third
Sunday in October).

NEARBY ATTRACTIONS:
The Barlow (food, wine,
and art complex on former
apple-processing site);
Russian River (rafting,
fishing, swimming,
canoeing, kayaking);
Laguna de Santa Rosa
(freshwater wetlands
with wildlife viewing);
California Carnivores
(botanical collection of
carnivorous plants).

onventional wisdom has it that great wines are made in the vineyard, the point being that although what winemakers do in the cellar is crucial, rigorous farming plays the outsize role. True enough, but as Emeritus Vineyards founder Brice Jones learned during four-plus decades of winegrowing, *where* one farms is even more significant. A former fighter pilot who started the Chardonnay powerhouse Sonoma-Cutrer in 1974, Jones used the proceeds from its 1999 sale to purchase the Hallberg Ranch, at the time an apple orchard. Jones and Kirk Lokka, his longtime vineyard manager, had hankered after the land for half a decade.

Entirely planted to Pinot Noir in 2000, the 115-acre ranch sits on a ridge whose sandy-loam soil, called Goldridge, drains well—Noir. Jones maintains that growing element: "cool summer nights, be-makes a wine complex." Hallberg's the mid-80s during the day, but drop them to the upper 40s.

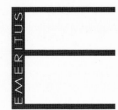

good conditions for growing Pinot great Pinot requires another key low 50°F, or you'll lose the acid that summer temperatures often reach fog rolls in nearly every evening to

As part of their ongoing quest to improve quality, Jones and Lokka switched to dry farming (without irrigation) in 2007. Lack of water forces the vines' roots to reach deeper into the soil, encountering more nutrients in the process. This adds further complexity to the wines, as do the eleven clones, or variants, of Pinot Noir planted, each imparting different fruit, floral, and flavor characteristics. David Lattin, who joined Emeritus in 2017 because of his admiration for Hallberg Ranch, isn't the only winemaker enamored of its grapes. The Hallberg Ranch Pinot Noir, on many top restaurants' wine lists, is Emeritus's standard-bearer. Lattin's counterparts from Gary Farrell, Chateau St. Jean, Joseph Jewell, and other wineries pay top dollar for the ranch's fruit.

Tastings at casual Emeritus are seated, and the wines are all estate-grown, dry-farmed Pinot Noirs from Hallberg and Pinot Hill Vineyard. The latter, located eight miles south, bedevils Lokka with its fog and wind, which can require even more viticultural attention than Hallberg. Pinot Hill's challenges and Hallberg's intriguing history—wine grapes were grown on the ranch before Prohibition—are among the topics of a winery tour that was voted the nation's best by *USA Today* readers.

The low-key excursion starts and ends in the lounge-like tasting space, an extension of a former Hallberg apple-processing structure that's decorated with apple-heyday mementos. Although the metal-frame building stands out amid the carpet of vineyards lining Gravenstein Highway, floor-to-ceiling folding glass windows put the visual emphasis on the ranch, all the more so on sunny days, when staffers open them to admit the same cooling breezes that nurture the grapes a few feet away.

FURTHERMORE WINES

Tasting room hosts at upbeat Furthermore Wines embark with guests on a "virtual road trip" down the California coast. The destinations: the state's premier appellations for cool-climate Pinot Noirs. These include Furthermore's home turf, the Russian River Valley and Sonoma Coast AVAs, as well as the Central Coast's Santa Lucia Highlands and Sta. Rita Hills AVAs.

Chad Richard and Robert Zeches, college best friends who created a tech company and other businesses in the 1990s, started Furthermore in 2006. Joining San Francisco's urban winery movement, they purchased grapes from respected growers and made wine—fifty cases' worth the first year—at custom-crush facilities in the city. As the wines earned positive critical notice, the duo gained access to fruit from Rosella's Vineyard in Santa Lucia, Gap's Crown in what is now the Petaluma Gap AVA, and other top sites.

In 2011, with production at about 2,000 cases, Furthermore purchased a three-acre Pinot Noir vineyard six miles from the Pacific Ocean in Occidental. Four years later, Richard and Zeches bought a second property, Sebastopol's Graton Ridge, along with its Chardonnay and Pinot Noir vines and winery. What's now the tasting room served as a farm stand and apple-processing space when apples were king along this stretch of Gravenstein Highway.

Furthermore achieved an additional milestone in 2015: the owners and their team received the Winemaker of the Year Award at the San Francisco International Wine Competition. In 2016 Richard and Zeches handed the winemaking reins to Sonoma County native Erica Stancliff. Stancliff's mentors include the internationally recognized consultant Paul Hobbs, for whom her mother worked for many years. When Stancliff was ten, Hobbs, whose namesake winery is a quarter mile south of Graton Ridge, asked her to describe the smells in a glass of Merlot. Impressed by her response, he asked her to take a sip. After hearing her observations, Hobbs told her she should become a winemaker. She took his advice, obtaining an enology degree at Fresno State University and later working for the winemaker in Argentina and elsewhere.

Richard also dates his passion for Pinot to his youth. "I decided to be a winemaker at the International Pinot Noir Conference in Oregon," he says. "I was there when I was nineteen years old with my father and a fake ID. I realized after tasting those wines that someday I would make Pinot Noir." To his great delight, in 2018 he and Zeches were invited by the conference—no deception required—to pour Furthermore wines for the first time, bringing worldwide attention to the enological journey visitors experience at a tasting here.

FURTHERMORE WINES
3541 Gravenstein Hwy. North
Sebastopol, CA 95472
707-823-3040
info@furthermorewines.com
furthermorewines.com

OWNERS: Chad Richard and Robert Zeches.

LOCATION: 4 miles north of downtown Sebastopol.

APPELLATIONS: Russian River Valley, Santa Lucia Highlands, Sta. Rita Hills, Sonoma Coast.

HOURS: 10 A.M.–4:30 P.M. daily.

TASTINGS: $20 for 5 wines.

TOURS: By appointment; impromptu requests subject to staff availability.

THE WINES: Chardonnay, Pinot Noir.

SPECIALTIES: Single-vineyard wines from California's top Pinot Noir appellations; Rosé of Pinot Noir; Alchemy (blend of Sonoma Coast Pinot Noirs).

WINEMAKER: Erica Stancliff.

ANNUAL PRODUCTION: 5,000 cases.

OF SPECIAL NOTE: Picnic area and bocce court. Wines available for purchase by glass and bottle to enjoy in picnic/bocce area. Winery is family and dog friendly. Most wines available only at tasting room.

NEARBY ATTRACTIONS: The Barlow (food, wine, and art complex on former apple-processing site); Russian River (rafting, fishing, swimming, canoeing, kayaking); Laguna de Santa Rosa (freshwater wetlands with wildlife viewing); California Carnivores (botanical collection of carnivorous plants).

GARY FARRELL VINEYARDS AND WINERY

GARY FARRELL VINEYARDS AND WINERY
10701 Westside Rd.
Healdsburg, CA 95448
707-473-2909
concierge@
garyfarrellwinery.com
garyfarrellwinery.com

FOUNDER: Gary Farrell.

LOCATION: 12 miles southwest of downtown Healdsburg, near Wohler Bridge.

APPELLATION: Russian River Valley.

HOURS: 10 A.M.–4 P.M. daily.

TASTINGS: By appointment.

TOURS: By appointment.

THE WINES: Chardonnay, Pinot Noir.

SPECIALTIES: Vineyard-designated Chardonnay and Pinot Noir.

WINEMAKER: Theresa Heredia.

ANNUAL PRODUCTION: 25,000 cases.

OF SPECIAL NOTE: Sweeping view of Russian River Valley. Limited-production wines available only at winery.

NEARBY ATTRACTIONS: Russian River (rafting, canoeing, kayaking, swimming, fishing); Armstrong Redwoods State Natural Reserve (hiking, horseback riding).

A sharp turn off Westside Road leads up a driveway that climbs four hundred feet in elevation past native live oaks, madrones, and towering redwoods to one of the Russian River Valley AVA's continuing success stories. On many summer mornings, this short journey from the Russian River's northern bank transports visitors above the fog that glides in from the Pacific, enveloping rows of Chardonnay and Pinot Noir grapes on both sides of the river. Valley views stretching south, east, and west from the Gary Farrell tasting spaces and broad terrace create an enchanting backdrop for enjoying small-production, single-vineyard wines from these varietals.

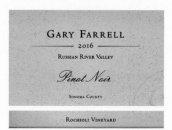

The winery's namesake founder was among the first vintners to recognize the Russian River Valley's poten- tial for producing outstand- ing Chardonnay and Pinot Noir. Farrell sold the winery more than a decade ago, but it still benefits from the rela- tionships he established with renowned grape growers in Sonoma County and beyond. Theresa Heredia, a chemist turned winemaker known for taking calculated risks in harvesting, fermentation, and aging, crafts dynamic wines with grapes from Gap's Crown, Rochioli, Allen, Hallberg, Bacigalupi, and other storied vineyards. The soil types of these vineyards vary, but their climates are generally the same, with morning and late-afternoon Pacific breezes and fog tempering the midday summer heat. Such conditions result in a longer ripening period, which helps the grapes develop richer flavors and retain proper acidity levels.

Heredia, who previously worked at Joseph Phelps Freestone Vineyards making Pinot Noir, likes to pick her grapes earlier than many of her Russian River Valley counterparts to avoid what she feels are the overly fruity characteristics that occur when berries are held too long on the vine. Her Pinots are vibrant yet reined in, her ideal Chardonnays "flinty, lemony, and savory," as she puts it.

Guests sample the impressive Gary Farrell lineup by appointment only at casually elegant seated tastings hosted by the winery's ambassadors and estate sommelier, who are well versed in the wines and the winery's lore. Given the consistency of both the climatic conditions and Heredia's winemaking style, a tasting here provides the opportunity to compare and contrast different vintages and vineyards and, particularly with the Pinot Noirs, the clones, or variants of the varietal. Subtly diverse, these wines are as beguiling as the setting itself.

HARTFORD FAMILY WINERY

Toyon, oak, and coast redwood fringe the sinuous country road that leads to the home of Hartford Family Winery. At the driveway, a one-lane bridge crosses Green Valley Creek into a forest clearing where the château-style winery offers a peaceful retreat. Sycamores shade the stately complex, and a fountain bubbles opposite the double doors of the tasting room. Furnished with European antiques, the spacious foyer opens into a space with crisp white cabinetry and a French limestone floor.

Renowned for crafting single-vineyard Chardonnay, Pinot Noir, and old-vine Zinfandel, the winery was founded in 1993 by Don and Jennifer Hartford. Don, whose family farmed strawberries in western Massachusetts, had recently concluded a successful law practice in Northern California and was drawn to the viticulture of Russian River Valley. With help from Jennifer's father, Jess Jackson, cofounder of Kendall-Jackson Wine Estates, the couple purchased the winery property about a dozen miles northwest of Santa Rosa.

Of the winery's fourteen Pinot Noir offerings, twelve are strikingly diverse single-vineyard bottlings made from 95 percent estate fruit. The estate vineyards thrive in seven appellations: Los Carneros, Anderson Valley, Sonoma Coast, Russian River Valley, Green Valley, Sta. Rita Hills, and Willamette Valley. All are cool-climate sites that yield small crops of often late-ripening grapes treasured for their flawless varietal flavors. The Far Coast Pinot Noir is sourced from estate vineyards located in Annapolis, on the Sonoma coast, some thirty miles north of the tasting room. For Chardonnay, the winery turns to the Sonoma Coast and Russian River Valley appellations. About 90 percent of the fruit is harvested from estate vineyards, including Fog Dance Vineyard, in the Green Valley AVA, and Seascape Vineyard, a six-acre ridgetop site facing Bodega Bay. The Hartfords craft five single-vineyard and one blended Zinfandel, all from dry-farmed Russian River Valley vines boasting an average age of a hundred-plus years. The grapes from these august vines exhibit rich berry and spice components born of both the vines' great age and the region's relatively chilly, protracted growing season.

The single-vineyard wines are made in limited lots, some as small as a hundred cases. During harvest, all the fruit is handpicked and then sorted by hand to remove everything but the best berries. Using only French oak barrels, the winemaker selects from nineteen different cooperages, matching barrels to each lot of wine to elevate the expression of both vineyard site and varietal characteristics.

HARTFORD FAMILY WINERY
8075 Martinelli Rd.
Forestville, CA 95436
707-887-8030
info@hartfordwines.com
hartfordwines.com

OWNERS: Don and Jennifer Hartford.

LOCATION: 2 miles northwest of Forestville.

APPELLATIONS: Anderson Valley, Green Valley, Los Carneros, Russian River Valley, Sonoma Coast, Sta. Rita Hills, Willamette Valley.

HOURS: 10 A.M.–4:30 P.M. daily.

TASTINGS: $25 for 6 wines. Additional tasting options available on website by reservation.

TOURS: None.

THE WINES: Chardonnay, Pinot Noir, Port, Rosé, Syrah, Zinfandel.

SPECIALTIES: Single-vineyard Chardonnay, Pinot Noir, and old-vine Zinfandel.

WINEMAKER: Jeff Stewart.

ANNUAL PRODUCTION: 12,000–15,000 cases.

OF SPECIAL NOTE: Shaded picnic area with tables. Zinfandel Port and most single-vineyard wines available only in tasting room. Second tasting room located at 331 Healdsburg Ave., Healdsburg, open 10:30 A.M.–5 P.M. daily.

NEARBY ATTRACTIONS: Russian River (rafting, fishing, swimming, canoeing, kayaking); Armstrong Redwoods State Reserve (hiking, horseback riding); Laguna de Santa Rosa (freshwater wetlands with wildlife viewing).

JORDAN VINEYARD & WINERY

JORDAN VINEYARD & WINERY
1474 Alexander Valley Rd.
Healdsburg, CA 95448
707-431-5250
800-654-1213
info@jordanwinery.com
jordanwinery.com

OWNER: John Jordan.

LOCATION: About 4 miles northeast of Healdsburg.

APPELLATIONS: Alexander Valley, Russian River Valley.

HOURS: 8 A.M.–4:30 P.M. Monday–Friday; 9 A.M.–3:30 P.M. Saturday and Sunday. Closed on Sundays December–March.

TASTINGS: $35 for Library Tasting of 3 wines, by appointment.

TOURS: $45 for Winery Tour and Library Tasting year-round. $125 for Estate Tour and Tasting Thursday–Monday May–October only. Both by appointment.

THE WINES: Cabernet Sauvignon, Chardonnay.

SPECIALTIES: Alexander Valley Cabernet Sauvignon, Russian River Valley Chardonnay.

WINEMAKER: Rob Davis.

ANNUAL PRODUCTION: 100,000 cases.

OF SPECIAL NOTE: Extensive landscaped grounds and gardens, including Tuscan olive trees. Jordan estate extra-virgin olive oil sold at winery. Same winemaker since 1976. Library and large-format wines available only at winery.

NEARBY ATTRACTIONS: Lake Sonoma (boating, camping, fishing, hiking, swimming); Jimtown Store (country market, homemade foods).

A sense of change amid permanence prevails at Jordan Vineyard & Winery, where the son of its founders has honored their legacy by adding new luster to this Alexander Valley icon. John Jordan was still a boy when his parents, Tom and Sally Jordan, established a reputation for meticulous winemaking. From the start, the couple took the high road, hiring André Tchelistcheff, Napa Valley's most esteemed winemaker in the 1970s, as their consulting enologist. To design their château and winery, they brought in the San Francisco architectural firm of Backen, Arrigoni & Ross, whose later projects included filmmaker George Lucas's Skywalker Ranch.

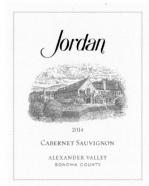

With its classic carmine doors and shutters, the château serves as a visual metaphor for the Jordan winemaking philosophy, which in the French tradition emphasizes balance, elegance, and food affinity. It is by design that Jordan Cabernet Sauvignons and Chardonnays grace the wine lists of many top restaurants. As was the case when the château was completed in 1976, the wines are still crafted by Rob Davis, the Jordans' original winemaker. However, numerous initiatives undertaken by John Jordan since he took the winery's helm in 2005 have reenergized both the winemaking and the hospitality. From advancements in fruit sourcing, oak aging, precision farming, and conserving natural resources to diversifying agriculture and creating new visitor experiences, Jordan maintains a relentless quest to improve with every vintage.

Visitors to Jordan can learn about its wines and history at tastings and on tours. Depending on the chosen experience, guests visit a wood-paneled private library and its cleverly hidden adjoining room, taste current and library wines as well as extra-virgin olive oil made from estate-grown olives, and sample small bites created by longtime executive chef Todd Knoll. The Winery Tour visits part of the château and passes by massive, highly sculptural oak tanks.

On the splurge-worthy Estate Tour and Tasting, participants sample fine pastries and briefly visit the winery before a Mercedes coach whisks them to an organic garden on the nearly 1,200-acre estate to view and taste the impressive produce. A lakeside oak grove is the setting for Chardonnays and light morsels, and a hilltop vista point provides an appropriately dramatic venue for tasting a current and a library Cabernet Sauvignon, matched with an array of food-pairing delicacies.

JOSEPH JEWELL

The aha moment that sparked vintner Adrian Jewell Manspeaker's infatuation with wine occurred during a night on the town for his twenty-fifth birthday. At dinner he splurged on a bottle from the year of his birth, a wine whose grapes, he learned from the label, were harvested the very week he was born. As he read the description more closely, it dawned on him, he recalls, "that every wine is more than just a Cabernet or Pinot Noir. There's a vintage. What happened that year? When were the grapes harvested? What winery made it? Who was the winemaker? What's the *story*?"

A year or so later, Manspeaker met Micah Joseph Wirth, who as the son of a winemaker was well acquainted with wines and their stories. After the two formed a wine-tasting group, Manspeaker's interest deepened further, prompting Wirth, then working at Gary Farrell Vine- yards and Winery, to ask if Manspeaker wanted to make wine with him. Their first effort, a Russian River Valley Pinot Noir made in a garage with equipment borrowed from Gary Farrell and other sources, placed second in a blind tasting of wines by two dozen far more accomplished producers.

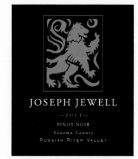

Buoyed by the encourage- ment of winemakers soon to become their peers, the duo set out in 2007 to establish a brand whose name joins its founders' middle ones. As a winery with no vineyards of its own, Joseph Jewell, which specializes in single-vineyard Russian River Valley Pinot Noirs, relies on strong relationships with premier growers, among them the owners of Hallberg Ranch, Bucher, and Starscape. The small operation also produces wines from Humboldt County, where Manspeaker was born. With fewer than two hundred acres of vineyards in the entire county, Humboldt wines qualify as California rarities.

Although Joseph Jewell also makes Chardonnay, Zinfandel, and a Rosé, the Russian River Val- ley Pinots, most crafted in small lots, are the winery's stars. Hosts, sometimes including one of the winemakers, pour them at a modest storefront tasting room along laid-back Forestville's short main drag. Two good tasting options are one showcasing the appellation wines and another featuring single- vineyard wines. For a more in-depth experience, guests can schedule tours of Starscape Vineyard led by Manspeaker or Wirth, with lunch included if desired. Starscape is also the tasting stop on the ultimate tour: a helicopter ride over the winery's main Russian River vineyards. In the air or on the ground, the Joseph Jewell story — best conveyed by the wines themselves — revolves around a passion for producing what Manspeaker hopes guests will agree are "killer Pinots from high-quality fruit."

JOSEPH JEWELL
6542 Front St.
Forestville, CA 95436
707-820-1621
adrian@josephjewell.com
josephjewell.com

OWNER: Adrian Manspeaker.

LOCATION: 12 miles west of Santa Rosa and 13 miles south of Healdsburg.

APPELLATIONS: Dry Creek Valley, Humboldt County, Russian River Valley.

HOURS: 11 A.M.–5 P.M. Thursday; 11 A.M.–7 P.M. Friday and Saturday; 11 A.M.–5 P.M. Sunday and Monday.

TASTINGS: $15 for Discover Flight of 4 wines; $25 for Single Vineyard Flight of 4 wines.

TOURS: Gourmet Picnic Lunch & Vineyard Tour ($52.50 per person); Luxury Helicopter Vineyards Tour with Winemaker ($500 per couple). Both by appointment.

THE WINES: Chardonnay, Pinot Gris, Pinot Noir, Syrah, Zinfandel.

SPECIALTY: Vineyard- designate Pinot Noirs.

WINEMAKERS: Adrian Jewell Manspeaker and Micah Joseph Wirth.

ANNUAL PRODUCTION: 2,500 cases.

OF SPECIAL NOTE: Open house events in April and October. Food-and-wine pairing (reserve two days ahead). Tasting room is pet friendly. On-site art gallery with works by Sonoma County painters and photographers. Gem Series Pinot Noirs available only in tasting room.

NEARBY ATTRACTION: Russian River (rafting, canoeing, kayaking, swimming, fishing).

KENWOOD VINEYARDS

KENWOOD VINEYARDS
9592 Sonoma Hwy.
(Hwy. 12)
Kenwood, CA 95452
707-282-4228
info@kenwoodvineyards
.com
kenwoodvineyards.com

OWNER:
Pernod Ricard USA.

LOCATION: 11 miles north
of downtown Sonoma, 13
miles east of Santa Rosa.

APPELLATIONS: Alexander
Valley, Dry Creek Valley,
Russian River Valley,
Sonoma Coast, Sonoma
Mountain, Sonoma Valley.

HOURS: 10 A.M.–5 P.M. daily.

TASTINGS: Classic Tasting,
$15 for 4 wines. Vintner's
Choice, 90+ points, single
vineyard, $25 for 5 wines.

TOURS: None.

THE WINES: Cabernet Sauvi-
gnon, Chardonnay, Merlot,
Pinot Gris, Pinot Noir,
Sauvignon Blanc, Syrah,
Zinfandel.

SPECIALTIES: Artist Series
Cabernet Sauvignon; wines
from Sonoma County
appellations; various single-
vineyard wines from author
Jack London's former estate.

WINEMAKER: Pat Henderson.

ANNUAL PRODUCTION:
650,000 cases.

OF SPECIAL NOTE: Wines
reflect diversity of Sonoma
County climates and ter-
rain. Many small-lot wines
available only in tasting
room.

NEARBY ATTRACTIONS:
Annadel State Park (hiking,
biking); Quarryhill
Botanical Garden (Asian
plant collection); Sugarloaf
Ridge State Park (hiking,
camping, horseback riding).

A weathered redwood barn erected by Italian brothers John and Amandio Pagani in 1906 still catches the eye as visitors proceed along the driveway that leads to historic Kenwood Vineyards. When San Franciscan Mike Lee and three relatives bought the Pagani Bros. operation in 1970, it was the last pre-Prohibition winery in the small town of Kenwood still selling wine bearing its owners' name. The neighbors who'd remained in business were selling grapes or wine in bulk to Gallo and other large producers. At the renamed Kenwood Vineyards, Lee focused on making premium wines and within a few years had garnered a reputation for quality Cabernet Sauvignon, Zinfandel, and especially Sauvignon Blanc. Along with several other newcomer wineries, the group contributed significantly to Sonoma County's winemaking renaissance.

In 1976 Kenwood tapped into literary history by contracting with the heirs of Jack London to make an exclusive line of wines from 130 acres of grapevines thriving in the red volcanic soils of the writer's beloved Beauty Ranch in nearby Glen Ellen. The Jack London Vineyard wines—sep- arate Cabernet Sauvi- gnon, Merlot, Syrah, and Zinfandel bottlings bearing distinctive wolf labels—are still made today, with some of the proceeds used to support the adjacent 1,400-acre Jack London State Park, where the writer is buried.

Kenwood made history of its own by launching the highly praised Artist Series. Always crafted from the winery's best lots of Cabernet Sauvignon, the series has included label artwork by Charles Mingus III, Pablo Picasso, and Alexander Calder. The Artist Series got off to a controversial start with the 1975 vintage, whose label of a nude reclining on a vineyard hillside was rejected by the federal gov- ernment for being "obscene and indecent." (The painting graced the 1994 vintage without incident.)

The current head winemaker, Pat Henderson, who got his start as an intern during the 1983 harvest and succeeded Lee in 2003, represents a link to Kenwood's roots. As Lee did, Henderson makes the wines cuvée style, with the grapes from each vineyard pressed (to release the juice), fermented, and aged separately to retain the lot's individual flavors. Based on those flavors, the winemaker determines the correct blend just before bottling. Until completion of a new tasting room, tastings will continue to take place where they have for decades, inside the humble, concrete-floored barn that got things rolling for the Pagani brothers a century ago.

La Rochelle Winery

A recent Sonoma County arrival with a fascinating backstory, La Rochelle makes more small-lot single-vineyard Pinot Noirs from more appellations than any winery in North America. Vintner Chuck Easley achieves La Rochelle's stylistic focus—producing complex age-worthy Pinot Noirs and Chardonnays—by sourcing grapes from seventeen unique California vineyards from Mendocino's Anderson Valley in the north to the Santa Lucia Highlands of the Central Coast. Sites capable of producing complex age-worthy Pinot Noirs are rare, Easley contends, using mushrooms and truffles as an analogy. "Mushrooms are wonderful and reasonably priced so we can enjoy them every day," he says. "Truffles require the perfect location, climate, and expertise to create something rare and cherished by connoisseurs." Grapes for La Rochelle's small-lot Pinot Noirs, Chardonnays, Pinot Meunier, and La Vie sparkling wine come from such special vineyards.

Sourcing from so many diverse growing conditions pro- create Polyphony, La Rochelle's the most delicate of wine grapes, prestigious vineyards with such vided Easley the opportunity to most intricate wine. Being among Pinot Noir lends itself to the building of layers of flavor and complexity, with each location's soil, clone types, and weather making a singular contribution. Easley describes Polyphony as "the culmination of what we do."

Easley purchased La Rochelle from his longtime friend Steven Mirassou. Mirassou, part of the seventh generation of America's oldest winemaking family, stewarded La Rochelle after E&J Gallo acquired Mirassou Winery. La Rochelle's wine club, started by the Mirassou family back in the 1960s, represents the evolution of the nation's first such winery club.

A powder-blue 1947 Willys pickup marks the short driveway leading to La Rochelle. Most tastings take place not in the modest indoor space, but outdoors on a patio whose picnic tables face a broad lawn, a vegetable garden, estate Chardonnay grapes, and a koi pond covered with lily pads. Hens and their chicks roam the two-and-a-half-acre property. Easley and his hospitality team pride themselves on an oft-heard comment from guests: "This feels like the old days, tasting in someone's backyard and meeting the people who actually make the wine." Tastings range from an introduction to La Rochelle's Pinot Noirs to the Reserve Experience, an excellent choice for guests interested in expanding their wine knowledge. To delve even deeper, make a reservation for the Polyphony Experience, whose participants learn how yeast, clones, vineyard location, and grower knowledge all contribute to the character, ageability, and complexity of Pinot Noir.

La Rochelle Winery
1233 Adobe Canyon Rd.
Kenwood, CA 95452
707-302-8000
info@lrwine.com
lrwine.com

Owner: Chuck Easley.

Location: Off Sonoma Hwy. (Hwy. 12), 1 mile north of Kenwood business district.

Appellations: Anderson Valley, Arroyo Seco, Bennett Valley, Los Carneros, Mendocino Ridge, Petaluma Gap, Russian River Valley, Santa Cruz Mountains, Santa Lucia Highlands, Sonoma Coast, Sonoma Valley, Sonoma Mountain.

Hours: 11 a.m.–5 p.m. daily.

Tastings: $20 for introductory tasting of 5 wines, reservation recommended. $50 for Reserve Tasting of 5 wines; $250 for Polyphony–Pinot Noir Experience of 12 wines.

Tours: None.

The Wines: Chardonnay, Pinot Meunier, Pinot Noir.

Specialties: Small-lot single-vineyard Pinot Noirs and Chardonnays; La Vie sparkling wine.

Winemaker: Chuck Easley.

Annual Production: 2,200 cases.

Of Special Note: Most wines available only in tasting room.

Nearby Attractions: Annadel State Park (hiking, biking); Quarryhill Botanical Garden (Asian plant collection); Sugarloaf Ridge State Park (hiking, camping, horseback riding).

LANDMARK VINEYARDS

LANDMARK VINEYARDS
101 Adobe Canyon Rd.
Kenwood, CA 95452
707-833-0053
info@landmarkwine.com
landmarkwine.com

OWNERS: Stewart and
Lynda Resnick.

LOCATION: Off Hwy. 12,
12 miles north of historic
Sonoma Plaza.

APPELLATIONS: Los Carneros,
Russian River Valley, Santa
Lucia Highlands, Santa
Maria Valley, Sta. Rita Hills,
Sonoma Coast, Sonoma
Valley, Monterey County,
San Benito County.

HOURS: 10 A.M.–5 P.M. daily.

TASTINGS: $20 for 5 wines at
bar; $30 for seated tasting
of single-vineyard wines;
$40 for groups of 6 or more,
by reservation.

TOURS: Estate Tour & Tasting
($40), 11 A.M. and 2 P.M.,
daily, by appointment.
Horse Drawn Carriage Tour
(free), May–September,
Saturday noon–3 P.M.

THE WINES: Chardonnay,
Pinot Gris, Pinot Noir.

SPECIALTIES: Small-
production vineyard-
designated wines.

WINEMAKER: Greg Stach.

ANNUAL PRODUCTION:
35,000 cases.

OF SPECIAL NOTE: Courtyard
area for picnics and tasting.
Bocce ball court. Private
Tower Tastings ($50) of
reserve wine in tower with
360-degree view. Annual
events include Half Shells &
Chardonnay Festival (May);
Pig, Pizza & Pinot Festival
(July); Harvest Festival
(October). Many vineyard-
designated wines available
only in tasting room. Second
tasting room featuring
Landmark wines located at
historic Hop Kiln winery.

This longtime local favorite sits along busy Highway 12 in Kenwood, but visitors often remark that its hacienda-style facility has the feel of a secluded vacation home. Valley oaks and poplars shade the landscaped outdoor courtyard, which faces eastward away from the highway toward Sugarloaf Ridge, the Mayacamas Mountains landform that dominates this section of northern Sonoma Valley. Especially on weekends, when the sounds of guests picnicking or playing cornhole and bocce ball fill the air, the place takes on a festive mood, but any day of the week this is a fine spot to enjoy Chardonnays and Pinot Noirs poured by knowledgeable, enthusiastic staffers.

Roses, wisteria, purple and white star jasmine, and other flowering plants provide seasonal splashes of color in the courtyard, with a large pond, a tall aquamarine fountain, and the nearby ridge the focal points. Following the winery's 1989 relocation here from nearby Windsor, many guests assumed that Sugarloaf repre- sented the titular landmark, but the name preceded the move. For the current owners, the name reflects their commitment to producing wines from landmark California vineyards, among them Sangiacomo, Rayhill, and Rodgers Creek in Sonoma County; Escolle Road in Monterey County; and Bien Nacido in Santa Barbara County.

Landmark's successful quest for quality grapes can be experienced up and down its lineup in leisurely tastings either in the courtyard or in the tall-ceilinged, Mexican-tiled indoor space. Overlook Chardonnay, the company's flagship wine, often scores well in blind tastings against pricier offerings, though given its stellar Sonoma County sources this isn't all that surprising. Winemaker Greg Stach displays an appropriately light touch with the several other Chardonnays, allowing the specific vineyard characteristics—the minerality of Sonoma Coast's Flocchini, for example, or the fruitier tendencies of Sangiacomo and Bien Nacido—to find expression in the wines. Stach shows equal finesse crafting the Pinot Noirs, whose stars include two midprice entrants, Santa Lucia Highlands (Monterey County) and Grand Detour (Sonoma Coast), along with the single-vineyard Rayhill (Russian River Valley) and Escolle Road (Santa Lucia Highlands) wines.

In 2016 Landmark took title on a bona fide landmark, the old Hop Kiln winery in Healdsburg. Built by Italian stonemasons in 1905 for use drying beer hops, the structure is considered the finest of its type still extant. Grapes for some of the Russian River's most noteworthy Chardonnays and Pinot Noirs are grown along Hop Kiln's stretch of Westside Road (trailblazing Rochioli is right next door), so Landmark's stature is only likely to increase as releases from these vineyards enter its portfolio.

LANDMARK VINEYARDS, HOP KILN ESTATE

From downtown Healdsburg near Highway 101, Westside Road follows the western banks of the Russian River as it flows through verdant vineyards, orchards, and farmland toward the Pacific Ocean. In the heart of this pastoral region—where grapes for some of the Russian River Valley's most noteworthy Chardonnays and Pinot Noirs are grown—an impossible-to-miss landmark suddenly looms on the scene: a majestic structure with three towering chimneys.

The impressive building—a local, state, and national historic landmark—is the Walters Hop Kiln, built in 1905. At the time, hops were California's third-largest crop. Ranch owner Sol Walters hired Angelo "Skinny" Soldini  to construct the massive stone and redwood building, which his crew finished in just thirty-five days. It consisted of three stone kilns for drying hops and an attached wooden cooling barn with a two-story press for baling. The hops traveled via a conveyer-belt tramway system up to the chimneys for heat- ing. Once dried, the hops were pulled into a cooling room below.

Starting in the 1940s, the demand for hops decreased. By the 1960s, vineyards, which had existed in the region since the late 1800s, had replaced most of the hops fields. This was the case at the Hop Kiln Estate, whose subsequent owners revived vineyards and planted new vines on the 240-acre ranch. In 2004 Westside Grapes LLC purchased the Hop Kiln Estate and replaced existing vineyards with ultra-premium vines—Pinot Noir (75 acres), Chardonnay (15.4 acres), and Pinot Gris (2.3 acres)—to make their own wines under the HKG (Hop Kiln Grown) label. The owners also sold grapes to a number of highly respected wineries, including Landmark Vineyards, based in Kenwood.

Landmark was very impressed with the quality of the fruit and coveted the property to produce estate wines and to preserve the historic hop kiln structure, considered the finest of its type still extant. Landmark owners Stewart and Lynda Resnick purchased the 240-acre Hop Kiln Estate in January 2016 and began extensive restorations of the kilns. In 2018 Landmark released its first Hop Kiln Estate Pinot Noir Reserve; it plans to introduce additional limited-production Hop Kiln Estate vintages steadily in the coming years.

The tasting room at the Hop Kiln Estate is in the historic stone and redwood hop building, in the cooling room beneath the chimneys. Here guests can sample the full range of Landmark wines at a long stainless-steel tasting bar that overlooks a peaceful pond and estate vineyards. Visitors are welcome to picnic outdoors, in a shaded courtyard by the entrance or by the pond, surrounded by bucolic Russian River Valley scenes.

LANDMARK VINEYARDS, HOP KILN ESTATE
6050 Westside Rd.
Healdsburg, CA 95448
707-433-6491
concierge@landmarkwine.com
landmarkwine.com

OWNERS: Stewart and Lynda Resnick.

LOCATION: 6 miles southwest of downtown Healdsburg.

APPELLATIONS: Los Carneros, Russian River Valley, Sonoma Coast, Santa Lucia Highlands, Santa Maria Valley, Sta. Rita Hills, Sonoma Coast, Sonoma Valley, Monterey County, San Benito County.

HOURS: 10 A.M.–5 P.M. daily.

TASTINGS: $20 for 6 wines.

TOURS: None.

THE WINES: Chardonnay, Pinot Gris, Pinot Noir.

SPECIALTIES: Small-production vineyard-designate wines.

WINEMAKER: Greg Stach.

ANNUAL PRODUCTION: 35,000 cases.

OF SPECIAL NOTE: Tasting room located in national historic landmark. Winery is family friendly. Picnic areas with cornhole set available with wine purchase. Cheeses, charcuterie, and accoutrements available for purchase. Build a Picnic Basket, $40, offering choice of meat, cheese, spread, and crackers, along with borrowed basket, blanket, cheese board with knives, and wineglasses, for on-site picnic. Many vineyard-designate wines available only in tasting room. Landmark sister tasting room located in Kenwood.

NEARBY ATTRACTIONS: Lake Sonoma; Russian River; Healdsburg Museum and Historical Society.

MOSHIN VINEYARDS

MOSHIN VINEYARDS
10295 Westside Rd.
Healdsburg, CA 95448
707-433-5499
moshin@moshinvineyards
.com
moshinvineyards.com

OWNERS: Rick Moshin
and family.

LOCATION: 10 miles southwest of Healdsburg.

APPELLATION: Russian River
Valley.

HOURS: 11 A.M.–4:30 P.M.
daily.

TASTINGS: $20 for 5 wines
(waived with purchase).

TOURS: By appointment
($30, includes tasting).

THE WINES: Chardonnay,
Merlot, Pinot Noir, Sauvignon Blanc, Zinfandel.

SPECIALTIES: Small-lot
vineyard-designated Pinot
Noirs, Perpetual Moshin
(Bordeaux blend), Moshin
Potion No. 11 (white
dessert wine).

WINEMAKER: Rick Moshin.

ANNUAL PRODUCTION:
9,000 cases.

OF SPECIAL NOTE: Russian
River Valley's only four-
tier gravity-flow winery.
Picnic area. Art gallery
with works by local and
other Northern California
artists. Events include
quilting show (winter) and
Barrel Tasting (March).
Most wines available only
in tasting room.

NEARBY ATTRACTIONS:
Armstrong Redwoods
State Natural Reserve
(hiking, horseback riding);
Russian River (rafting,
fishing, swimming,
canoeing, kayaking).

Westside Road out of downtown Healdsburg follows the mild curves of the Russian River past vineyards of mostly Chardonnay and Pinot Noir grapes. About ten miles southwest of town, both road and river bend sharply, and a colorful, far-larger-than-life sculpture of a hummingbird drawing nectar from a flower hovers in midair, marking the short, secluded driveway that ends at the Moshin Vineyards tasting room. Fronted by weathered redwood reclaimed from the century-old barn of a neighboring property, the room and the winery behind it nuzzle into the surrounding hillside so comfortably that it may come as a surprise to learn both were completed in 2005.

The winery and the wines vision of Rick Moshin, a for- passion for Pinot Noir wines tion to every aspect of their of the Russian River Valley, makers to appear in their wines with visitors, but those made within it represent the mer math instructor whose is exceeded only by his atten- creation. In this placid portion it's not unheard of for wine- tasting rooms to discuss their lucky enough to stop here when Moshin is around might also hear him describe the intricacies of the energy-saving four-tier gravity-flow winery he designed, how he helped lay its foundation and build it, and how he milled and finished the sensually smooth tongue-and-groove black walnut tasting bar.

Sometimes a tasting bar is just a tasting bar, but in this case it provides clues about the artistry, precision, and scholarship that inform Moshin's lineup of a dozen-plus small-lot Pinot Noirs. They, along with Pinot Blanc, Chardonnay, Zinfandel, and other wines, are made from grapes grown on twenty-eight estate acres and sourced from noted, mostly Sonoma County growers. Moshin, who started his wine brand in 1989, tends to pick Pinot Noir grapes on the early side to preserve the acidity, a European approach that often produces wines that pair well with food and age gracefully. They're also lower in alcohol than many of their Russian River counterparts.

Moshin's ultimate goal is to create affordable wines whose flavors—from the fruit, oak fermentation, tannins, and, most importantly, soil and climate—blend harmoniously. At tastings the choices include a few whites and, if available, a pale but zesty Rosé of Pinot Noir. The flavors of the Pinot Noirs range from the light and floral to bolder expressions of the varietal. The convivial, well-informed pourers share entertaining anecdotes about the wines, the winery, and the Russian River Valley appellation. The mood is so welcoming that in fine weather many guests extend their stay at the picnic tables near Rufus, the sculptural hummingbird, who's often joined by real ones flitting by.

PAPAPIETRO PERRY

A passion for Pinot Noir has connected Ben Papapietro and Bruce Perry for nearly forty years. Both grew up in San Francisco, in Italian and Portuguese families who always served wine at meals and gatherings. Their grandfathers made wine at home in the basement, and the young boys watched and listened, learning the basic techniques of the craft. They also developed a keen, lifelong interest in cooking and wine.

As a young man, Ben Papapietro sampled various Burgundian wines and fell in love with Pinot Noir. Purchasing this varietal for daily consumption, however, would certainly break the family bank. So he began making his own wines at home in the garage, following his ancestral tradi-tions. In the 1970s, while working at the San Francisco Newspaper Agency, he became friends with Bruce Perry, who sampled and liked Papapietro's garage-made wines and joined in on the endeavor. After producing several varietals, they knew it was Pinot Noir that won their hearts. Burt Williams, who worked at the San Francisco Newspaper Agency, was also an avid home winemaker. In the early 1980s,

Williams cofounded Williams Selyem, a Sonoma winery famed for its Pinot Noir production. Ben and Bruce worked there during annual harvests and honed their winemaking skills.

More than a decade later, the two friends felt ready to introduce their Pinot Noir to the public. They located a winemaking facility in Sonoma County and founded Papapietro Perry Winery in 1998. Bruce and Ben eventually left their day jobs and dove full force into the business, with Bruce and Ben making the wine and Bruce's wife, Renae, running the business. Later, Ben's wife, Yolanda, joined to handle distributor relations.

The devoted attention paid off quickly, as Papapietro Perry wines have consistently earned high praise and awards from critics since the early 2000s. Ben Papapietro's winemaking skills have also garnered acclaim among Pinot Noir devotees. Today the winery produces ten Pinot Noirs and a small amount of Zinfandel and Chardonnay. Grapes come from established vineyards in the Russian River Valley, as well as surrounding Dry Creek Valley, Anderson Valley, and the Sonoma Coast.

The Papapietro Perry tasting room opened in 2005 at Timber Crest Farms, in the heart of pastoral Dry Creek Valley. The former farm now houses a collection of wineries and other small businesses. Visitors taste wines at a gleaming copper-topped bar made of intricately woven barrel staves, which Bruce Perry built by hand. In many ways, the unpretentious space reflects the winery's homey, but humble beginnings in the family garage more than three decades past.

PAPAPIETRO PERRY
4791 Dry Creek Rd.
Healdsburg, CA 95448
877-GO-PINOT
707-433-0422
info@papapietro-perry
.com
papapietro-perry.com

OWNERS: Bruce and Renae Perry, Ben and Yolanda Papapietro.

LOCATION: 4.7 miles northwest of Healdsburg.

APPELLATIONS: Anderson Valley, Dry Creek Valley, Russian River Valley, Sonoma Coast.

HOURS: 11 A.M.–4:30 P.M. daily.

TASTINGS: $15 for 4 wines. Pinot on the Patio wine-and-cheese tasting by appointment.

TOURS: None.

THE WINES: Chardonnay, Pinot Noir, Rosé, Zinfandel.

SPECIALTY: Pinot Noir.

WINEMAKER:
Ben Papapietro.

ANNUAL PRODUCTION:
6,000–8,000 cases.

OF SPECIAL NOTE: Covered patio with tables and views of Dry Creek Valley; picnic area; bocce ball. Annual events include Winter Wineland (January), Passport to Dry Creek Valley (April), Chardonnay and Lobster (July), and Wine and Food Affair (November).

NEARBY ATTRACTIONS:
Lake Sonoma (hiking, fishing, boating, camping, swimming); Russian River (swimming, canoeing, kayaking, rafting, fishing); Healdsburg Museum and Historical Society (exhibits about Sonoma County); Hand Fan Museum (collection of antique fans).

PATZ & HALL

PATZ & HALL
21200 8th St. East
Sonoma, CA 95476
707-265-7700
info@patzhall.com
patzhall.com

OWNER: Ste. Michelle Wine Estates.

LOCATION: 3 miles southeast of historic Sonoma Plaza.

APPELLATIONS: Sonoma Valley, Sonoma Coast, Green Valley of Russian River Valley, Los Carneros, Russian River Valley, Mendocino.

HOURS: 10 A.M.–4 P.M. daily.

TASTINGS: $35 for 4 wines, held on the hour; $75 for Salon tasting of 6 reserve wines paired with food, by appointment.

TOURS: None.

THE WINES: Chardonnay, Pinot Noir, sparkling wine.

SPECIALTIES: Vineyard-designated Chardonnay and Pinot Noir.

WINEMAKER: James Hall.

ANNUAL PRODUCTION: 40,000 cases.

OF SPECIAL NOTE: Vineyard-view patio with seating, fountain, and large lawn with games. Gifts, jewelry, and wine-themed items available for purchase. Outdoor events monthly June–September. Annual events include Spring Release Open House (two Saturdays in March) and Fall Release Party (first Saturday in October). Many wines available only in tasting room.

NEARBY ATTRACTIONS: Historic buildings in downtown Sonoma; bike rentals; Vella Cheese Company.

The Sonoma House, the gleaming Patz & Hall hospitality center, sits amid lush vineyards in the rural east side of the town of Sonoma. For nearly a decade, the winery tasting room had been located in a modest office building near the city of Napa. When sixteen acres with a single-family residence became available up the road from its Sonoma winemaking facility, Patz & Hall seized the opportunity to transform the estate property into a one-of-a-kind wine country complex. The goal was to have a number of indoor and outdoor areas where the winery could welcome customers and get to know them in person. The Sonoma House opened to the public in early 2014 following an extensive remodel that preserved the feel of a family home while adding contemporary flair and furnishings.

Patz & Hall was estab-  lished in 1988 by four individuals — Donald Patz, James Hall, Anne Moses, and Heather Patz — who dedicated themselves to making benchmark wines sourced from distinctive California vineyards. Today, they produce a total of twenty Chardonnays and Pinot Noirs, all without owning a single vineyard themselves. Patz & Hall was founded on an unusual business model that began in the 1980s at Flora Springs Winery & Vineyards, when assistant winemaker James Hall and national sales manager Donald Patz forged a close friendship. Their mutual enthusiasm for wine produced from elite, small vineyards inspired them to blend their talents along with those of Anne Moses and Heather Patz. Together, the team boasted a wealth of knowledge and experience gleaned at such prestigious Northern California wineries as Far Niente, Girard Winery, and Honig Winery, where Hall was once the winemaker.

The founders applied their specialized expertise and daily attention to different areas of the winery's operations. The cornerstone of Patz & Hall is this integrated, hands-on approach, combined with close personal relationships with growers who supply them with fruit from outstanding family-owned vineyards.

Visitors to The Sonoma House can sit on leather stools at the marble tasting bar, where casual tasting takes place, or can join a private, hour-long tasting, paired with food, in the elegant Sonoma House Salon. Guided tastings are also held on the shaded outdoor terrace. Over the course of an hour or more, guests sample single-vineyard wines paired with local farmstead cheeses and other light fare. Visitors are welcome to sink into comfortable sofas and chairs by a roaring fire in the living room in winter, or in fair weather in oversize rattan chairs on the terrace or back lawns, where they enjoy stunning views of the Mayacamas Mountains and estate vineyards.

TASTING ROOM
OPEN FROM 10-4:30

NO
BUSSES
PLEASE

PARKING

RAVENSWOOD WINERY

RAVENSWOOD WINERY
18701 Gehricke Rd.
Sonoma, CA 95476
707-933-2332
888-669-4679
ravenswoodwinery.com

OWNER:
Constellation Brands.

LOCATION: About .5 mile northeast of the town of Sonoma via Fourth St. East and Lovall Valley Rd.

APPELLATION: Sonoma Valley.

HOURS: 10 A.M.–4:30 P.M. daily.

TASTINGS: $25 for vineyard-designated wines.

TOURS: 10:30 A.M. daily ($30).

THE WINES: Bordeaux-style blends, Cabernet Franc, Cabernet Sauvignon, Chardonnay, Icon (Zinfandel, Carignane, Petite Sirah, Alicante Bouschet), Moscato, Petite Sirah, Zinfandel.

SPECIALTY: Zinfandel.

WINEMAKER: Gary Sitton.

ANNUAL PRODUCTION: 500,000 cases.

OF SPECIAL NOTE: Blending seminars by appointment. Bicyclists and other visitors are welcome to picnic on stone patio with view of vineyards.

NEARBY ATTRACTIONS: Mission San Francisco Solano, Lachryma Montis (Mariano Vallejo's estate), and other historic buildings in downtown Sonoma; bike rentals; Vella Cheese Company; Sonoma Cheese Factory; Sonoma Traintown (rides on a scale railroad).

Few wineries set out to make cult wines, and probably fewer earn a widespread following as well. Ravenswood has done both. Its founders began by crushing enough juice to produce 327 cases of Zinfandel in 1976, and although the winery also makes other wines, Zinfandel remains king. Nearly three-quarters of Ravenswood's production is Zinfandel.

Cofounder Joel Peterson and chairman and cofounder Reed Foster were so successful with that first, handcrafted vintage that they have had to live up to the standard it set ever since. Ravenswood produces represent the spectrum of the ranging from peppery and spicy is one common denominator, it is the winery in 1990: "No Wimpy

fourteen different Zinfandels that varietal's personality, with tastes to chocolaty and minty. If there reflected in the slogan adopted by Wines."

Most of Ravenswood's grapes independent growers. It is those ensure the consistency of the wines. The Strotz family invited Joel Mountain vineyard, which they had come from more than a hundred long-standing relationships that One vineyard source dates to 1886. Peterson to visit their Sonoma named Pickberry because of all the wild blackberries harvested there. Peterson immediately recognized the quality of the Strotz grapes, and in 1988 Ravenswood released the first of its many blends of Cabernet Sauvignon, Cabernet Franc, and Merlot under the vineyard-designated name Pickberry.

Peterson never set out to specialize in Zinfandel; originally he was more interested in the Bordeaux varietals he began tasting at the age of ten with his father, Walter, founder of the San Francisco Wine Sampling Club. In time, however, he fell under the spell of Zinfandel. In the 1970s, after a brief career as a wine writer and consultant, he went to work for the late Joseph Swan, considered one of California's outstanding craftsmen of fine Zinfandel. Thus the stage was set for the varietal's ascendancy at the winery Peterson founded.

Ravenswood farms fourteen acres of estate vineyards on the northeast side of Sonoma. The old stone building, once home to the Haywood Winery, has extensive patio seating with beautiful south-facing views of the vineyards. Thanks to the company's growth, the winemaking operations have since been relocated to a 45,000-square-foot facility in Carneros, to the south, but the tasting room remains. Originally a cozy, even cramped affair, it was greatly expanded in 1996, and now has plenty of elbow room as well as ample natural light for visitors who come to sample and appreciate the wines.

SBRAGIA FAMILY VINEYARDS

SBRAGIA FAMILY VINEYARDS
9990 Dry Creek Rd.
Geyserville, CA 95441
707-473-2992, ext.107
info@sbragia.com
sbragia.com

OWNER: Ed Sbragia.

LOCATION: Northern end of Dry Creek Rd.

APPELLATIONS: Dry Creek Valley, Howell Mountain, Moon Mountain District Sonoma County, Mt. Veeder, Napa Valley, Russian River Valley.

HOURS: 10:30 A.M.–5 P.M. daily.

TASTINGS: $20 for 5 wines (walk-ins welcome). Other experiences by reservation.

TOURS: Vine to Bottle tour of estate vineyard and wine cellar daily at 10 A.M. (reservation required).

THE WINES: Cabernet Sauvignon, Carignane, Chardonnay, Merlot, Petite Sirah, Sauvignon Blanc, Zinfandel.

SPECIALTIES: Vineyard-designate Chardonnay and Cabernet Sauvignon from Sonoma County and Napa Valley.

WINEMAKER: Adam Sbragia.

ANNUAL PRODUCTION: 12,000 cases.

OF SPECIAL NOTE: Several wines available only in tasting room. All Cabernet Sauvignons made since 2001 available for tasting by special request. Winery is dog friendly. Family among the first to plant vineyards in Dry Creek Valley. Second tasting room located in downtown Sonoma.

NEARBY ATTRACTIONS: Lake Sonoma (hiking, fishing, boating, camping, swimming); Russian River (swimming, canoeing, kayaking, rafting, fishing).

Just before Dry Creek Road reaches its western terminus at Lake Sonoma, Sbragia Family Vineyards winery, perched on a hill, comes into view. Visitors approach the winery on a winding driveway that passes through Zinfandel vineyards and lush gardens. Among the features they first see is the generous terrace overlooking the vineyards. The setting is an ideal one for an afternoon of tasting and enjoying the vista from the top of Dry Creek Valley.

Sbragia Family Vineyards is many miles from the place where Ed Sbragia gained acclaim during his thirty years of making award-winning wines at Beringer Vineyards in the Napa Valley before retiring in 2008. Seven years

before he left Beringer, he started producing wine under the Sbragia Family Vineyards label. Perhaps even more important, Ed had begun passing on his vast knowledge of viticulture and enology to his son Adam, who worked as assistant winemaker at Beringer under his dad. These days at Sbragia, the roles are reversed: Adam is the winemaker, and Ed, as he puts it, "just helps out."

The family's roots grow deep in this part of Sonoma County. After purchasing land in Dry Creek Valley, the Sbragias grew and dried plums there for years. By the early 1960s, Ed's father, Gino Sbragia, had planted grapevines, which Ed helped tend until he went off to study chemistry at the University of California, Davis, and then earn an enology degree at Fresno State. Gino Sbragia, who died in 1995, had tried to start a winery, but Prohibition and the Great Depression prevented him from realizing his dream. Ed promised his father that he would eventually establish a winery of his own.

Sbragia Family Vineyards, admired for its Zinfandels and bold, polished Cabernet Sauvignons, focuses on vineyard-designate wines. Several, including a Chardonnay, a Sauvignon Blanc, a Merlot, and some Zinfandels, are grown on estate vineyards. A vineyard owned by Ed's uncle provides fruit for another Zinfandel, and Gamble Ranch in Napa Valley, one of Ed's favorite vineyards, supplies Chardonnay. Fruit for five Sbragia Cabernet Sauvignons comes from various mountaintop properties: Andolsen Vineyard in Dry Creek Valley and Monte Rosso Vineyards in the Moon Mountain District, in Sonoma County; and, in the Napa Valley, Godspeed Vineyard on Mount Veeder and the Hughes and Neal vineyards on Howell Mountain. Of the estate vineyards, two are named in honor of Gino Sbragia. Gino's Vineyard was planted to Zinfandel more than six decades ago. La Promessa, also producing Zinfandel, acknowledges Ed's fulfilled promise to his father.

STONE EDGE FARM WINERY

A labor of joy and consummate teamwork, Stone Edge Farm is geared toward collectors of premium Cabernet Sauvignon. Private tastings take place at the winery's Silver Cloud Vineyard, 1,800 feet above the Sonoma Valley floor in the remote Moon Mountain District AVA. Silver Cloud lies down a narrow road that traverses the Mayacamas Mountains between Sonoma Valley's Glen Ellen and Oakville in the Napa Valley. Just getting here can be an adventure, but for most guests the transition to ease and relaxation commences before they enter the 160-acre property's 1920s farmhouse. Painted in muted green and gray, the home merges with the valley and coast live oaks, Japanese maples, and garden plants that surround it. This fetching tableau, viewed at most tastings from a salvaged-pine trestle table in the home's former living room, might enhance any well-made wine, but here the reverse happens: intricate Cabernets elevate winemaker Jeff Baker's intricate Cabernets elevate the experience substantially. Baker, who has been crafting sophisticated wines from these parts since the 1970s, extols Moon Mountain fruit for the intensity that its volcanic ash soils impart.

Baker creates two estate-grown red wines each vintage, the Stone Edge Farm Cabernet Sauvignon and the Surround Red Bordeaux Blend. Most of the grapes for these balanced, complex wines come from Silver Cloud and Baker's Mount Pisgah Vineyard five miles away, with additional fruit from Stone Edge Vineyard, the valley-floor estate of winery owners John "Mac" McQuown and his wife, Leslie. The latter grapes, from the alluvial soils of the property's prehistoric riverbed, add velvety, almost voluptuous notes. Phil Coturri, dubbed the Wizard of Green by *Wine Spectator* magazine for his three-plus decades of organic agricultural practices, farms all three vineyards.

Stone Edge Farm's wines aren't distributed to shops or restaurant lists, with one exception: Edge, the winery's private club in downtown Sonoma. The extensive organic culinary garden at Stone Edge Vineyard supplies olive oil, fruit, herbs, honey, and more than 150 heirloom vegetables for the dishes of culinary director John McReynolds, whose credits include cofounding the popular Cafe La Haye across the street and a three-year stint as filmmaker George Lucas's executive chef.

A polymath and lifelong wine collector, Mac McQuown upended the financial-industry status quo nearly a half century ago when a Wells Fargo team he led developed the world's first stock index fund. He cofounded Monterey County's Chalone Wine Group and later collaborated with Baker on a different Moon Mountain project. Stone Edge Farm represents their mutual desire to produce world-class Bordeaux-style wines, showcased to discerning collectors in a casually luxurious setting.

STONE EDGE FARM ESTATE VINEYARDS & WINERY
P.O. Box 487
Sonoma, CA 95476
707-935-6520
concierge@stoneedgefarm.com
stoneedgefarm.com

OWNERS: Mac and Leslie McQuown.

LOCATION: 30-minute drive north of downtown Sonoma.

APPELLATIONS: Moon Mountain District, Sonoma Valley.

HOURS: Monday–Saturday, by appointment.

TASTINGS: $75–$95.

TOURS: Tastings include tour of winery, barn, gardens, and farmhouse.

THE WINES: Cabernet Sauvignon, Sauvignon Blanc.

SPECIALTIES: Estate-grown Cabernet Sauvignon from organically farmed vineyards.

WINEMAKER: Jeff Baker.

ANNUAL PRODUCTION: 3,500 cases.

OF SPECIAL NOTE: All wines available only through the winery. Edge, the winery's culinary home and club in downtown Sonoma, offers seasonal lunches, private dining, and culinary classes, by appointment. The award-winning *Stone Edge Farm Cookbook*, by Stone Edge culinary director John McReynolds, is available at all the winery's properties and on the winery's website.

NEARBY ATTRACTIONS: Jack London State Historic Park (hiking, historic sites, horseback tours); Quarryhill Botanical Garden (Asian plant collection).

THREE STICKS WINES

THREE STICKS WINES
143 W. Spain St.
Sonoma, CA 95476
707-996-3328, ext. 105
concierge@threestickswines
.com
threestickswines.com

OWNERS: Bill and Eva Price.

LOCATION: Half block west of
Sonoma Plaza's northwest
corner.

APPELLATIONS: Sonoma
Mountain, Sonoma Coast,
Russian River Valley.

HOURS: 10 A.M.–5 P.M.
Monday–Saturday, by
appointment only.

TASTINGS: $40 for 4 current-
release wines, $80 for
7 library and current-
release wines. Food-and-
wine pairings and private
luncheon by appointment.

TOURS: Guided tours of
historic Vallejo-Casteñada
Adobe included with tasting.

THE WINES: Chardonnay,
Pinot Noir.

SPECIALTIES: Small-lot, single-
vineyard Chardonnays and
Pinot Noirs.

WINEMAKER: Bob Cabral.

ANNUAL PRODUCTION:
5,000 cases.

OF SPECIAL NOTE: Adobe with
tasting salon is the oldest
occupied residence in
Sonoma. Original garden
designed by landscape ar-
chitect and gardening writer
and editor Helen Van Pelt
in 1948. Casteñada Rhône
blends available only at the
Adobe.

NEARBY ATTRACTIONS:
Mission San Francisco
Solano and other historic
buildings in downtown
Sonoma; bike rentals; Vella
Cheese Company; Sonoma
Cheese Factory; Sonoma
Traintown (rides on a scale
railroad).

Bob Cabral, who in 2009 crafted the first 100-point Pinot Noir in North America for the elite Williams Selyem Winery in Healdsburg and two years later was named *Wine Enthusiast* winemaker of the year, created a buzz in early 2015 when he signed on with the smaller, newer Three Sticks Wines. One attraction of the boutique operation for Cabral was the opportunity to make Chardonnays and Pinot Noirs, his specialties, from Durell, Gap's Crown, and Walala, three legendary Sonoma Coast vineyards of the winery's owner, Bill Price. Cabral cited as another lure the chance "to get my hands purple again," focusing on artisanal winemaking instead of juggling the business side as well.

In addition to its estate vine- yards, Three Sticks sources fruit for other Pinots and Chardonnays from equally noteworthy locales. Though best known for its Pinots, the winery received high praise from *Wine Spectator* and other publications for the 2015 Chardon- nays, the first vintages entirely under Cabral's control.

The Three Sticks tasting salon is located steps west of Sonoma Plaza in an 1842 adobe, one of Sonoma's old- est structures. Following a painstaking restoration, Ken Fulk, a San Francisco–based celebrity designer, created an understatedly exuberant interior space that evokes California's period of Mexican rule (1822–1846) through its textures and earth tones, yet feels emphatically au courant.

The Adobe's place in Sonoma history and the town's role in ushering in the modern era of California winemaking, which began a few miles away at Buena Vista Winery in 1857, are among the topics discussed at seated tastings limited to eight participants. The exclusive sessions, some of which involve locally sourced cuisine designed to pair with the wines, include a tour of the Adobe and its garden, whose lush vegetation provides a backdrop for contemporary elements—fountains, a fire pit, and two arbors fashioned of willow branches supported by thick reclaimed Douglas fir beams. Depending on the weather and guests' preferences, tastings unfold either inside the Adobe at a handcrafted elm table or outside in the garden at a cast-stone one.

While Price was a principal in an investment company with wine holdings that included Chateau St. Jean in Kenwood, he developed a passion for Pinot Noir that eventually inspired the creation of Three Sticks. One might assume the origins of the winery's name are grape related, but they actually derive from his high school days in Hawaii as a surfer. His fellow surfers dubbed him "Billy Three Sticks," after the Roman numerals in his full name, Bill Price III.

Napa and Sonoma Wine Varietals

The wineries in this book currently produce the following wines, as well as many unique proprietary blends. Before you visit a tasting room to sample or purchase a particular wine variety, contact the winery to make sure it is available.

CABERNET FRANC
Anderson's Conn Valley
    Vineyards
B. Wise Vineyards
Clos Du Val
Goosecross Cellars
Madrigal Family Winery
Peju
Ravenswood Winery
Silverado Vineyards
St. Supéry Estate Vineyards
    & Winery
Trinchero Napa Valley

CABERNET SAUVIGNON
Acumen
Amista Vineyards
Anderson's Conn Valley
    Vineyards
B Cellars Vineyards
    and Winery
B. Wise Vineyards
Beaulieu Vineyard
Bennett Lane Winery
Beringer Vineyards
Cast Wines
Chateau St. Jean
Cliff Lede Vineyards
Clos Du Val
Conn Creek Napa Valley
Frank Family Vineyards
Goosecross Cellars
Grgich Hills Estate
The Hess Collection Winery
Jordan Vineyard & Winery
Kenwood Vineyards
Laird Family Estate

Madrigal Family Winery
Materra | Cunat Family
    Vineyards
Peju
The Prisoner Wine
    Company
Quixote Winery
Ravenswood Winery
Robert Mondavi Winery
Rombauer Vineyards
Sbragia Family Vineyards
Silverado Vineyards
St. Supéry Estate Vineyards
    & Winery
Stag's Leap Wine Cellars
Stags' Leap Winery
Sterling Vineyards
Stewart Cellars
Stone Edge Farm Winery
Trinchero Napa Valley
Whitehall Lane Winery
Yao Family Wines

CARIGNANE
Sbragia Family Vineyards

CHARBONO
The Prisoner Wine
    Company

CHARDONNAY
Amista Vineyards
Anderson's Conn Valley
    Vineyards
B Cellars Vineyards
    and Winery
B. Wise Vineyards

Beaulieu Vineyard
Bennett Lane Winery
Beringer Vineyards
Breathless Sparkling Wines
Cast Wines
Chateau St. Jean
Clos Du Val
Conn Creek Napa Valley
Donum Estate
Frank Family Vineyards
Furthermore Wines
Gary Farrell Vineyards
    and Winery
Goosecross Cellars
Grgich Hills Estate
Hartford Family Winery
The Hess Collection Winery

Jordan Vineyard & Winery
Joseph Jewell
Kenwood Vineyards
Laird Family Estate
La Rochelle Winery
Landmark Vineyards
Landmark Vineyards,
    Hop Kiln Estate
Materra | Cunat Family
    Vineyards
Moshin Vineyards
Papapietro Perry
Patz & Hall
Peju
The Prisoner Wine
    Company
Ravenswood Winery
Robert Mondavi Winery
Rombauer Vineyards
Sbragia Family Vineyards
Silverado Vineyards
St. Supéry Estate Vineyards
    & Winery
Stag's Leap Wine Cellars
Stags' Leap Winery
Sterling Vineyards
Stewart Cellars
Three Sticks Wines
Trinchero Napa Valley
Whitehall Lane Winery

CHENIN BLANC
The Prisoner Wine
   Company

FUMÉ BLANC
Chateau St. Jean
Grgich Hills Estate
Madrigal Family Winery
Robert Mondavi Winery

GEWÜRZTRAMINER
Chateau St. Jean
Madrigal Family Winery

GRENACHE
Amista Vineyards
Bella Vineyards and
   Wine Caves
Madrigal Family Winery

MALBEC
Chateau St. Jean
Conn Creek Napa Valley
The Hess Collection Winery
Laird Family Estate
Quixote Winery
Silverado Vineyards
St. Supéry Estate Vineyards
   & Winery
Stewart Cellars
Trinchero Napa Valley

MERLOT
Anderson's Conn Valley
   Vineyards
B Cellars Vineyards
   and Winery
Beaulieu Vineyard
Beringer Vineyards
Chateau St. Jean
Clos Du Val
Conn Creek Napa Valley
Goosecross Cellars

Grgich Hills Estate
Kenwood Vineyards
Materra | Cunat Family
   Vineyards
Moshin Vineyards
Peju
The Prisoner Wine
   Company
Robert Mondavi Winery
Rombauer Vineyards
Sbragia Family Vineyards
Silverado Vineyards
St. Supéry Estate Vineyards
   & Winery
Stag's Leap Wine Cellars
Stags' Leap Winery
Sterling Vineyards
Stewart Cellars
Trinchero Napa Valley
Whitehall Lane Winery

MOSCATO
Ravenswood Winery
Robert Mondavi Winery
St. Supéry Estate Vineyards
   & Winery

MOURVÈDRE
Amista Vineyards

PETIT VERDOT
Clos Du Val
Madrigal Family Winery
Peju
Silverado Vineyards
St. Supéry Estate Vineyards
   & Winery
Trinchero Napa Valley

PETITE SIRAH
B Cellars Vineyards
   and Winery
B. Wise Vineyards
Bella Vineyards and
   Wine Caves
Cast Wines
Frank Family Vineyards
Goosecross Cellars
The Hess Collection Winery
Madrigal Family Winery
Materra | Cunat Family
   Vineyards
Ravenswood Winery
Quixote Winery
Sbragia Family Vineyards
Stags' Leap Winery
Trinchero Napa Valley

PINOT BLANC
Chateau St. Jean

PINOT GRIGIO
Laird Family Estate

PINOT GRIS
Joseph Jewell
Kenwood Vineyards
Landmark Vineyards
Landmark Vineyards,
   Hop Kiln Estate

PINOT MEUNIER
La Rochelle Winery

PINOT NOIR
Anderson's Conn Valley
   Vineyards
B Cellars Vineyards
   and Winery
B. Wise Vineyards
Breathless Sparkling Wines
Cast Wines
Chateau St. Jean
Clos Du Val
Domaine Carneros
Donum Estate
Emeritus Vineyards
Frank Family Vineyards
Furthermore Wines
Gary Farrell Vineyards
   and Winery
Goosecross Cellars
Hartford Family Winery
Joseph Jewell
Kenwood Vineyards
Laird Family Estate
La Rochelle Winery
Landmark Vineyards
Landmark Vineyards,
   Hop Kiln Estate
Moshin Vineyards
Papapietro Perry
Patz & Hall
Robert Mondavi Winery
Sterling Vineyards
Stewart Cellars
Three Sticks Wines
Whitehall Lane Winery

PORT
Frank Family Vineyards
Hartford Family Winery
Madrigal Family Winery

RIESLING
Chateau St. Jean

ROSATO DI SANGIOVESE
Silverado Vineyards

ROSÉ
Breathless Sparkling Wines
Cast Wines
Emeritus Vineyards
Furthermore Wines
Hartford Family Winery
Madrigal Family Winery
Papapietro Perry
Peju
Stags' Leap Winery

SANGIOVESE
B Cellars Vineyards
   and Winery
Frank Family Vineyards
Silverado Vineyards

SAUVIGNON BLANC
Acumen
Anderson's Conn Valley
   Vineyards
B Cellars Vineyards
   and Winery
Beaulieu Vineyard
Cast Wines
Cliff Lede Vineyards
Clos Du Val
Conn Creek Napa Valley

Goosecross Cellars
The Hess Collection Winery
Kenwood Vineyards
Laird Family Estate
Materra | Cunat Family
   Vineyards
Moshin Vineyards
Peju
Rombauer Vineyards
Sbragia Family Vineyards
Silverado Vineyards
St. Supéry Estate Vineyards
   & Winery
Stag's Leap Wine Cellars
Sterling Vineyards
Stewart Cellars
Stone Edge Farm Winery
Trinchero Napa Valley
Whitehall Lane Winery
Yao Family Wines

SÉMILLON
Silverado Vineyards
St. Supéry Estate Vineyards
   & Winery
Trinchero Napa Valley

SPARKLING WINE
Amista Vineyards
Breathless Sparkling Wines
Cast Wines
Domaine Carneros
Frank Family Vineyards
Laird Family Estate
La Rochelle Winery
Mumm Napa
Patz & Hall
Sterling Vineyards

SYRAH
Amista Vineyards
B Cellars Vineyards
   and Winery
B. Wise Vineyards
Bella Vineyards
   and Wine Caves
Chateau St. Jean
Goosecross Cellars
Hartford Family Winery
Joseph Jewell
Kenwood Vineyards
Laird Family Estate
Materra | Cunat Family
   Vineyards

TANNAT
B. Wise Vineyards

TEMPRANILLO
Madrigal Family Winery

VIOGNIER
Chateau St. Jean
The Hess Collection Winery
Materra | Cunat Family
   Vineyards
Stags' Leap Winery

ZINFANDEL
Amista Vineyards
B Cellars Vineyards
   and Winery
B. Wise Vineyards
Bella Vineyards
   and Wine Caves
Cast Wines
Frank Family Vineyards
Grgich Hills Estate
Hartford Family Winery
The Hess Collection Winery
Joseph Jewell
Kenwood Vineyards
Madrigal Family Winery
Moshin Vineyards
Papapietro Perry
The Prisoner Wine
   Company
Ravenswood Winery
Rombauer Vineyards
Sbragia Family Vineyards
Silverado Vineyards
Sterling Vineyards

ACKNOWLEDGMENTS

Creativity, perseverance, integrity, and commitment are fundamental qualities
for guaranteeing the success of a project. The artistic and editorial teams who worked
on this edition possess these qualities in large measures. My heartfelt thanks go to
Cheryl Crabtree and Daniel Mangin, writers; Robert Holmes, photographer;
Judith Dunham, copyeditor; Linda Bouchard, proofreader;
Poulson Gluck Design, production; Scott Runcorn, color correction;
and Ben Pease, cartographer.

In addition, I am grateful for the invaluable counsel and
encouragement of Chester and Frances Arnold; Olivia Atherton;
Estelle Silberkleit and William Silberkleit; Lisa Silberkleit;
Danny Biederman; and the scores of readers and winery
enthusiasts who have contacted me over the past decade
to say how much they enjoy this book series.

— Tom Silberkleit

Also available in e-book format for iPad, Kindle, Kobo, Nook, and other tablets.

Wine House Press
127 East Napa Street, Suite E, Sonoma, CA 95476
707-996-1741

Editor and publisher: Tom Silberkleit
Original design: Jennifer Barry Design
Production: Poulson Gluck Design
Copyeditor: Judith Dunham
Cartographer: Ben Pease
Color correction: Eviltron
Photo editing assistant: Frances Arnold
Proofreader: Linda Bouchard

All photographs by Robert Holmes, except the following:
page 29, bottom right: courtesy Bennett Lane Winery; page 32: Brent Miller; page 33, bottom right: courtesy Cliff Lede
Vineyards; page 34 and page 35: David Dines Photography; page 40 and page 41: Tubay Yabut; page 56: Brent Winebrenner;
page 75: courtesy Sterling Vineyards; page 78, bottom left: David Matheson; page 79: Michal Venera; page 80 and page 81:
Brent Miller; page 103: Kara Brodgesell; page 110, bottom left: Matt Armendariz, bottom right: Marina Martinez;
page 111: Matt Armendariz; page 113, bottom left: courtesy Helico Sonoma.

Front cover photograph: Vineyards on Silverado Trail, Napa Valley, CA
Back cover photographs: top left: Domaine Carneros; top right: Amista Vineyards;
bottom left: B Cellars Vineyards and Winery; bottom right: Robert Mondavi Winery.

Printed and bound in Singapore through Imago Sales (USA) Inc.
ISBN-13: 978-0-9853628-8-1

Ninth Edition

Distributed by Publishers Group West, 1700 Fourth Street, Berkeley, CA 94710, www.pgw.com

The publisher has made every effort to ensure the accuracy of the information contained in
The California Directory of Fine Wineries, but can accept no liability for any loss, injury, or inconvenience
sustained by any visitor as a result of any information or recommendation contained in this guide.
Travelers should always call ahead to confirm hours of operation, fees, and other highly variable information.

Always act responsibly when drinking alcoholic beverages by selecting a designated driver or prearranged transportation.

Customized Editions

Wine House Press will print custom editions of this volume for bulk purchase at your request. Personalized covers and
foil-stamped corporate logo imprints can be created in large quantities for special promotions or events, or as premiums.
For more information, contact Custom Imprints, Wine House Press, 127 E. Napa Street, Suite E, Sonoma, CA 95476; 707-996-1741.

Join the Facebook Fan Page: www.facebook.com/CaliforniaFineWineries
Follow us on Twitter: twitter.com/cafinewineries
Scan to visit our website: www.CaliforniaFineWineries.com